The Wiersbe

BIBLE STUDY SERIES

The
Wiersbe
BIBLE STUDY SERIES

MARK

Serving Others

as You Walk

with the

Master Servant

David C Cook®
transforming lives together

THE WIERSBE BIBLE STUDY SERIES: MARK
Published by David C Cook
4050 Lee Vance View
Colorado Springs, CO 80918 U.S.A.

David C Cook Distribution Canada
55 Woodslee Avenue, Paris, Ontario, Canada N3L 3E5

David C Cook U.K., Kingsway Communications
Eastbourne, East Sussex BN23 6NT, England

The graphic circle C logo is a registered trademark of David C Cook.

All Scripture quotations in this study are taken from the Holy Bible, New
International Version®, NIV®. Copyright © 1973, 1984 by Biblica, Inc.™ Used by
permission of Zondervan. All rights reserved worldwide. www.zondervan.com.

In the *Be Diligent* excerpts, unless otherwise noted, all Scripture quotations are taken
from the King James Version of the Bible. (Public Domain.) Scripture quotations
marked NASB are taken from the New American Standard Bible®, Copyright © 1960,
1995 by The Lockman Foundation. Used by permission. (www.Lockman.org).

All excerpts taken from *Be Diligent*, second edition, published by David C
Cook in 2010 © 1987 Warren W. Wiersbe, ISBN 978-1-4347-6631-1.

ISBN 978-0-7814-0843-1
eISBN 978-1-4347-0552-5

© 2013 Warren W. Wiersbe

The Team: Steve Parolini, Karen Lee-Thorp, Amy Konyndyk,
Nick Lee, Jack Campbell, Karen Athen
Series Cover Design: John Hamilton Design
Cover Photo: iStockPhoto

Printed in the United States of America
First Edition 2013

3 4 5 6 7 8 9 10 11

061815

Contents

Introduction to Mark

Meeting Needs

The gospel of Mark is just the book for busy people who want to use every opportunity to serve God. It presents our Lord "on the move," meeting the physical and spiritual needs of all kinds of people. Mark depicts Jesus as God's suffering Servant who came, not to be ministered to, but to minister—even to the extent of giving His life for us on the cross.

Our world is filled with hurting people who need our ministry. Jesus left His church on earth so that we might continue the ministry He started. However, I fear that in the church today, we have too many spectators and not enough participants, too many celebrities and not enough servants.

The Servant

Mark wrote for the Romans, and ultimately for all of us, and his theme is *Jesus Christ the Servant*. If we had to pick a key verse in this gospel, it would be Mark 10:45: "For even the Son of Man did not come to be served, but to serve, and to give his life as a ransom for many."

If our time together studying Mark's gospel encourages you to be diligent in your own ministry to others, then the time has not been wasted. May our Lord enable all of us to be servants for His glory!

—*Warren W. Wiersbe*

How to Use This Study

This study is designed for both individual and small-group use. We've divided it into eight lessons—each references one or more chapters in Warren W. Wiersbe's commentary *Be Diligent* (second edition, David C Cook, 2010). While reading *Be Diligent* is not a prerequisite for going through this study, the additional insights and background Wiersbe offers can greatly enhance your study experience.

The **Getting Started** questions at the beginning of each lesson offer you an opportunity to record your first thoughts and reactions to the study text. This is an important step in the study process as those "first impressions" often include clues about what it is your heart is longing to discover.

The bulk of the study is found in the **Going Deeper** questions. These dive into the Bible text and, along with helpful excerpts from Wiersbe's commentary, help you examine not only the original context and meaning of the verses but also modern application.

Looking Inward narrows the focus down to your personal story. These intimate questions can be a bit uncomfortable at times, but don't shy away from honesty here. This is where you are asked to stand before the mirror of God's Word and look closely at what you see. It's the place to take a good look at yourself in light of the lesson and search for ways in which you can grow in faith.

Going Forward is the place where you can commit to paper those things you want or need to do in order to better live out the discoveries you made in the Looking Inward section. Don't skip or skim through this. Take the time to really consider what practical steps you might take to move closer to Christ. Then share your thoughts with a trusted friend who can act as an encourager and accountability partner.

Finally, there is a brief **Seeking Help** section to close the lesson. This is a reminder for you to invite God into your spiritual-growth process. If you choose to write out a prayer in this section, come back to it as you work through the lesson and continue to seek the Holy Spirit's guidance as you discover God's will for your life.

Tips for Small Groups

A small group is a dynamic thing. One week it might seem like a group of close-knit friends. The next it might seem more like a group of uncomfortable strangers. A small-group leader's role is to read these subtle changes and adjust the tone of the discussion accordingly.

Small groups need to be safe places for people to talk openly. It is through shared wrestling with difficult life issues that some of the greatest personal growth is discovered. But in order for the group to feel safe, participants need to know it's okay *not* to share sometimes. Always invite honest disclosure, but never force someone to speak if he or she isn't comfortable doing so. (A savvy leader will follow up later with a group member who isn't comfortable sharing in a group setting to see if a one-on-one discussion is more appropriate.)

Have volunteers take turns reading excerpts from Scripture or from the commentary. The more each person is involved even in the mundane tasks, the more they'll feel comfortable opening up in more meaningful ways.

The leader should watch the clock and keep the discussion moving. Sometimes there may be more Going Deeper questions than your group can cover in your available time. If you've had a fruitful discussion, it's okay to move on without finishing everything. And if you think the group is getting bogged down on a question or has taken off on a tangent, you can simply say, "Let's go on to question 5." Be sure to save at least ten to fifteen minutes for the Going Forward questions.

Finally, soak your group meetings in prayer—before you begin, during as needed, and always at the end of your time together.

The Servant
(MARK 1)

Before you begin ...
- *Pray for the Holy Spirit to reveal truth and wisdom as you go through this lesson.*
- *Read Mark 1. This lesson references chapter 1 in* Be Diligent. *It will be helpful for you to have your Bible and a copy of the commentary available as you work through this lesson.*

Getting Started

From the Commentary

"The gospel is neither a discussion nor a debate," said Dr. Paul S. Rees. "It is an announcement!"

Mark wasted no time giving that announcement, for it is found in the opening words of his book. Matthew, who wrote primarily for the Jews, opened his book with a genealogy. After all, he had to prove to his readers that Jesus Christ is indeed the rightful Heir to David's throne.

Since Luke focused mainly on the sympathetic ministry of the Son of Man, he devoted the early chapters of his book to a record of the Savior's birth. Luke emphasized Christ's humanity, for he knew that his Greek readers would identify with the perfect Babe who grew up to be the perfect Man.

John's gospel begins with a statement about eternity. Why? Because John wrote to prove to the whole world that Jesus Christ of Nazareth is the Son of God (John 20:31). The *subject* of John's gospel is the deity of Christ, but the *object* of his gospel is to encourage his readers to believe on this Savior and receive the gift of eternal life.

—*Be Diligent*, page 17

1. Mark wrote his gospel for the Romans. How did the Romans differ from the audiences Matthew, Luke, and John intended to read their gospels? What announcement did Mark proclaim in his opening sentence? What key words stand out to you in that sentence that will likely be important later? The theme of Mark's gospel is "Jesus Christ the Servant." What sorts of readers would you expect to be interested in that theme?

More to Consider: Read Mark 10:45. How does this verse speak to the core of Mark's message?

2. Choose one verse or phrase from Mark 1 that stands out to you. This could be something you're intrigued by, something that makes you uncomfortable, something that puzzles you, something that resonates with you, or just something you want to examine further. Write that here.

Going Deeper

From the Commentary

The fact that Mark wrote with the Romans in mind helps us understand his style and approach. The emphasis in this gospel is on *activity*. Mark describes Jesus as He busily moves from place to place and meets the physical and spiritual needs of all kinds of people. One of Mark's favorite words is "straightway," meaning "immediately." He uses it forty-one times. Mark does not record many of our Lord's sermons because his emphasis is on what Jesus did rather than what Jesus said. He reveals Jesus as God's Servant, sent to minister to suffering people and to die for the sins of the world.

—*Be Diligent*, page 18

3. What effect do you think Mark's focus on "activity" has in chapter 1? What impression of Jesus comes across? Why did Mark omit a genealogy or an account of Jesus' birth? Why might those stories be less important to a Roman audience than to a Jewish one?

From the Commentary

John Mark, the author of this gospel, states boldly that Jesus Christ is the Son of God. It is likely that Mark was an eyewitness of some of the events that he wrote about. He lived in Jerusalem with his mother, Mary, and their home was a meeting place for believers in the city (Acts 12:1–19). Several scholars believe that Mark was the young man described in Mark 14:51–52. Since Peter called Mark "my son" (1 Peter 5:13), it is probable that it was Peter who led Mark to faith in Jesus Christ. Church tradition states that Mark was "Peter's interpreter," so that the gospel of Mark reflects the personal experiences and witness of Simon Peter.

—*Be Diligent*, page 18

4. Why is it important that the author of this gospel was an eyewitness to some of the events he recorded? The word *gospel* means "good news." What would the "good news" have been to the Romans reading Mark's book?

From Today's World

The gospel writers each had a target audience in mind. Matthew wrote to the Jews. Mark wrote to the Romans. If you look at churches in the modern age, you find a similar kind of customization in the approach they take. Some might be focused on reaching seekers. Some are dedicated to building leaders out of seasoned believers. Some reach out to the inner city, and others speak the language of the suburbs.

5. Why is it helpful for a church to tailor its approach to sharing the gospel? What are the benefits of narrowing your focus? What are the dangers?

From the Commentary

In his ongoing commentary on witnesses to Jesus the Servant, Mark cites two quotations from the Old Testament prophets, Malachi 3:1 and Isaiah 40:3 (note also Ex. 23:20). The words *messenger* and *voice* refer to John the Baptist, the prophet God sent to prepare the way for His Son (Matt. 3; Luke 3:1–18; John 1:19–34). In ancient times, before a king visited any part of his realm, a messenger was sent before him to prepare the way. This included both repairing the roads and preparing the people. By calling the nation to repentance, John the Baptist prepared the way for the Lord Jesus Christ. Isaiah and Malachi join voices in declaring that Jesus Christ is the Lord, Jehovah God.

Jesus called John the Baptist the greatest of the prophets (Matt. 11:1–15). In his dress, manner of life, and message of repentance, John identified with Elijah (2 Kings 1:8; Mal. 4:5; Matt. 17:10–13; and note Luke 1:13–17). The "wilderness" where John ministered is the rugged wasteland along the western shore of the Dead Sea. John was telling the people symbolically that they were in a "spiritual wilderness" far worse than the physical wilderness that their ancestors had endured for forty years. John called the people to leave their spiritual wilderness, trust their "Joshua" (Jesus), and enter into their inheritance.

—*Be Diligent*, page 19

6. Why was it important for Mark to include prophets in his list of witnesses to Jesus? What sort of king did John the Baptist prepare people to expect? How did he prepare them? How might the idea of "messengers" have resonated with the Romans?

From the Commentary

We expect a servant to be *under* authority and to *take* orders, but God's Servant *exercises* authority and *gives* orders—even to demons—and His orders are obeyed. Mark describes three scenes that reveal our Lord's authority as the Servant of God.

The first scene involves Jesus' temptation (Mark 1:12–13). Mark does not give as full an account of the temptation as do Matthew (4:1–11) and Luke (4:1–13), but Mark adds some vivid details that the others omit. The Spirit "driveth him" into the wilderness. Mark used this strong word eleven times to describe the casting out of demons. The New American Standard Version has it *impelled*, and the New International Version translates it *sent*. It does not suggest that our Lord was either unwilling or afraid to face Satan. Rather, it is Mark's way of showing the intensity of the experience. No time was spent basking in the glory of the heavenly voice or the presence of the heavenly dove. The Servant had a task to perform and He immediately went to do it.

In concise form, Mark presents us with two symbolic pictures. Our Lord's forty *days* in the wilderness remind us of Israel's forty *years* in the wilderness. Israel failed when they were tested, but our Lord succeeded victoriously. Having triumphed over the enemy, Jesus could now go forth and call a new people who would enter into their spiritual inheritance. Since the name *Jesus* is the Greek form of "Joshua," we can see the parallel.

The second picture is that of the "last Adam" (1 Cor. 15:45). The first Adam was tested in a beautiful Garden and failed, but Jesus was tempted in a dangerous wilderness and won the victory. Adam lost his "dominion" over creation because of his sin (Gen. 1:28; Ps. 8), but in Christ, that dominion has been restored for all who trust Him (Heb. 2:6–8). Jesus was with the wild beasts and they did not harm Him. He gave a demonstration of that future time of peace and righteousness, when the Lord shall return and establish His kingdom (Isa. 11:9; 35:9). Indeed, He is a Servant with authority!

—*Be Diligent*, pages 20–21

7. Review Mark 1:12–28. How does the temptation scene reveal Jesus' authority? Why was it important for Mark to establish Jesus' authority?

How might this approach to revealing Jesus' character have resonated with Mark's audience?

From the Commentary

> The second scene that reveals Jesus' authority involves His preaching (Mark 1:14–22). If ever a man spoke God's truth with authority, it was Jesus Christ (see Matt. 7:28–29). It has been said that the scribes spoke *from* authorities but that Jesus spoke *with* authority. Mark was not recording here the beginning of our Lord's ministry, since He had already ministered in other places (John 1:35—4:4). He is telling us why Jesus left Judea and came to Galilee: Herod had arrested John the Baptist, and wisdom dictated that Jesus relocate. By the way, it was during this journey that Jesus talked with the Samaritan woman (John 4:1–45).
>
> —*Be Diligent*, page 21

8. What is the difference between speaking with authority and speaking from authority? What was Jesus' main message (Mark 1:15)? How would you put it into your own words? (See also John 3:1–7.)

More to Consider: Jesus preached that people should repent (change their minds) and believe. (See Acts 20:21.) But He also taught that repentance alone was not enough. What does repentance without faith become? (See Matt. 27:3–5; 2 Cor. 7:8–10.)

From the Commentary

The third scene that reveals Jesus' authority involves His command (Mark 1:23–28). We wonder how many synagogue services that man had attended without revealing that he was demonized. It took the presence of the Son of God to expose the demon, and Jesus not only exposed him, but He also commanded him to keep quiet about His identity and to depart from the man. The Savior did not want, nor did He need, the assistance of Satan and his army to tell people who He was (see Acts 16:16–24).

The demon certainly knew exactly who Jesus was (see Acts 19:13–17) and that he had nothing in common with Him. The demon's use of plural pronouns shows how closely he was identified with the man through whom he was speaking. The demon clearly identified Christ's humanity ("Jesus of Nazareth") as well as His deity ("the Holy One of God"). He also confessed great fear that Jesus might judge him and send him to the pit.

—*Be Diligent*, page 24

9. Why is it significant that the demon knew who Jesus was? What's the difference between knowing who Jesus is and knowing Him? (See James 2:19.)

From the Commentary

Two miracles of healing are described in Mark 1:29–45, both of which reveal the compassion of the Savior for those in need. In fact, so great was His love for the needy that the Savior ministered to great crowds of people after the Sabbath had ended, when it was lawful for them to come for help. It would appear that God's Servant was at the beck and call of all kinds of people, including demoniacs and lepers, and He lovingly ministered to them all.

Jesus and the four disciples left the synagogue and went to Peter and Andrew's house for their Sabbath meal. Perhaps Peter was a bit apologetic because his wife had to care for her sick mother and was unable to entertain them in the usual manner. We do not know about the other disciples, but we do know that Peter was a married man (Mark 1:30).

Peter and Andrew not only brought their friends James and John home with them from the service, but they also brought the Lord home. That is a good example for us to follow: Don't leave Jesus at the church—take Him home with you and let Him share your blessings and your burdens. What a privilege it was for Peter and his family to have the very Son of God as a guest in their humble home. Before long, the Guest became the Host, just as one day the Passenger in Peter's boat would become the Captain (Luke 5:1–11).

By faith, the men told Jesus about the sick woman, no doubt expecting Him to heal her. That is exactly what He did! The fever left her immediately, and she was able to go to the kitchen and serve the Sabbath meal. If you have ever had a bad fever, then you know how painful and uncomfortable it is. You also know that after the fever leaves you, it takes time for you to regain your strength. But not so in this case! She was able to serve the Lord immediately. And isn't service to our Lord one of the best ways to thank Him for all He has done for us?

—*Be Diligent*, pages 25–26

10. Review Mark 1:29–45. What was the result of Jesus' miracle? How long did Jesus continue to heal people? Why is it notable that Mark distinguished between the demonized and the diseased (1:32)? What overall impression do you get of Jesus from this passage? From Mark 1 in general?

Looking Inward

Take a moment to reflect on all that you've explored thus far in this study of Mark 1. Review your notes and answers and think about how each of these things matters in your life today.

Tips for Small Groups: To get the most out of this section, form pairs or trios and have group members take turns answering these questions. Be honest and as open as you can in this discussion, but most of all, be encouraging and supportive of others. Be sensitive to those who are going through particularly difficult times and don't press for people to speak if they're uncomfortable doing so.

11. What is it about the theme of "Jesus as Servant" that resonates most with you? Why is it important to you to see Jesus as a Servant? What about that image is difficult for you?

12. What in Mark 1 helps you to see Jesus' authority? Why is His authority important to you? How do you experience Jesus' authority in your faith life?

13. Jesus' healing instantly created disciples willing and able to serve Him. What are some ways Jesus has enabled you to serve Him?

Going Forward

14. Think of one or two things that you have learned that you'd like to work on in the coming week. Remember that this is all about quality, not quantity. It's better to work on one specific area of life and do it well than to work on many and do poorly (or to be so overwhelmed that you simply don't try).

Do you want to trust and respond more to Jesus' authority? Be specific. Go back through Mark 1 and put a star next to the phrase or verse that is most encouraging to you. Consider memorizing this verse.

Real-Life Application Ideas: Take a few minutes to think about Jesus as a Servant. How does Jesus' servanthood affect your daily life? Where do you see His authority working in your life? Consider all the places where your faith touches daily living—at work, at home, in community. How does Jesus' life intersect with those places? If you discover places where Jesus is absent, look for ways to invite His presence into those aspects of your life through prayer, study, or simply being aware of Jesus' love.

Seeking Help

15. Write a prayer below (or simply pray one in silence), inviting God to work on your mind and heart in those areas you've noted in the Going Forward section. Be honest about your desires and fears.

Notes for Small Groups:

- *Look for ways to put into practice the things you wrote in the Going Forward section. Talk with other group members about your ideas and commit to being accountable to one another.*

- *During the coming week, ask the Holy Spirit to continue to reveal truth to you from what you've read and studied.*

- *Before you start the next lesson, read Mark 2:1—3:12. For more in-depth lesson preparation, read chapter 2, "What the Servant Offers You," in* Be Diligent.

Three Gifts
(MARK 2:1—3:12)

Before you begin …
- *Pray for the Holy Spirit to reveal truth and wisdom as you go through this lesson.*
- *Read Mark 2:1—3:12. This lesson references chapter 2 in* Be Diligent. *It will be helpful for you to have your Bible and a copy of the commentary available as you work through this lesson.*

Getting Started

From the Commentary

With amazing speed the news spread that a miracle-working Teacher had come to Capernaum, and wherever our Lord went, great crowds gathered. They wanted to see Him heal the sick and cast out demons. Had they been interested in His message of the gospel, these multitudes would have been an encouragement to Jesus, but He knew that most of them were shallow in their thinking and blind to their own needs. Often the Lord found it necessary to leave the city and go out into the wilderness to pray (Luke 5:15–16). Every servant of God should follow His example and take time away from people in order to meet the Father and be refreshed and revitalized through prayer.

Now the time had come for Jesus to demonstrate to the people what His ministry was all about. After all, He had come to do much more than relieve the afflictions of the sick and the demonized. Those miracles were wonderful, but there was something greater for the people to experience—they could enter into the kingdom of God! They needed to understand the spiritual lessons that lay behind the physical miracles He was performing.

—Be Diligent, page 31

1. What marked the change in Jesus' ministry—from healing the sick and delivering people from demons to teaching about the kingdom of God? How do you think Jesus' followers felt when they witnessed this shift? What surprised them about Jesus' bold teachings?

2. Choose one verse or phrase from Mark 2:1—3:12 that stands out to you. This could be something you're intrigued by, something that makes you uncomfortable, something that puzzles you, something that resonates with you, or just something you want to examine further. Write that here.

Going Deeper

From the Commentary

Whether the event in Mark 2:1–12 took place in His own house ("He was at home" NASB) or Peter's house is not made clear. Since hospitality is one of the basic laws of the East, the people of Capernaum did not wait for an invitation but simply came to the house in droves. This meant that some of the truly needy people could not get close enough to Jesus to receive His help. However, four friends of a palsied man decided to lower their friend through the roof, trusting that Jesus would heal him, and Jesus did. This miracle of healing gave our Lord the opportunity to teach an important lesson about forgiveness.

Consider this scene through the eyes of the Lord Jesus. When He *looked up*, He saw the four men on the roof with their sick friend. Houses had flat roofs that were usually accessible by means of an outside stairway. It would not be difficult to remove the tiles, laths, and grass that comprised the roof and make an opening large enough to fit their friend through on his mat.

We must admire several characteristics of these men, qualities that ought to mark us as "fishers of men." For one thing, they were deeply concerned about their friend and wanted to see him helped. They had the faith to believe that Jesus could and would meet his need. They did not simply "pray about it," but they put some feet to their prayers, and they did not permit difficult circumstances to discourage them. They worked together and dared to do something different, and Jesus rewarded their efforts. How easy it would have been for them to say, "Well, there is no sense trying to get to Jesus today! Maybe we can come back tomorrow."

—*Be Diligent*, page 32

3. Review Mark 2:1–12. What is most notable about Jesus' analysis of the paralyzed man? How was this healing dramatically different from previous healings? How did the religious leaders of the time respond to Jesus' handling of this situation? Why was this significant?

More to Consider: Read John 9:1–3. What does this passage reveal about the different causes of sickness? How is Jesus' response to this man's sins an example of His greatest miracle?

From the Commentary

> Jesus affirmed His deity not only by forgiving the man's sins and healing his body, but also by applying to Himself the title "Son of man." This title is used fourteen times in Mark's gospel, and twelve of these references are found after Mark 8:29, when Peter confessed Jesus as the Christ of God (Mark 2:10, 28; 8:31, 38; 9:9, 12, 31; 10:33, 45; 13:26, 34; 14:21, 41, 62). It was definitely a messianic title (Dan. 7:13–14), and the Jews would have interpreted it that way. Jesus used this title about eighty times in the Gospels.
>
> —*Be Diligent*, page 34

4. What might the religious leaders of the day have learned had they opened their hearts to Jesus' bold proclamation of forgiveness? How might that have changed the course of history? How did God use their hardened hearts to advance the narrative of Jesus' life story?

From the History Books

Over the years, the world has seen plenty of self-proclaimed messiahs. This dates back to even before Jesus arrived on the scene. Some were easily dismissed as lunatics, but others gained a following of a few or even many who chose to believe their claims. As recent as a couple of decades ago, the leader of the Branch Davidians, David Koresh, not only claimed the title of messiah, but he also led many of his followers to their deaths.

5. Why would anyone claim to be the messiah? What does such a claim say about the person? Why do people follow these self-proclaimed messiahs? What makes Jesus' story different? How might He have been initially viewed as "just another false prophet" by the Jews? What ultimately proved His messiahship?

From the Commentary

It soon became evident that Jesus was deliberately associating Himself with the outcasts of Jewish society. He even called a tax collector to become one of His disciples! We do not know that Levi was a dishonest man, though most of the tax collectors were, but the fact that he worked for Herod Antipas and the Romans was enough to disgrace him among loyal Jews. However, when Jesus called him, Levi did not argue or delay. He got up and followed Jesus, even though he knew that Rome would never give him back his job. He burned his bridges ("And he left everything behind," Luke 5:28 NASB), received a new name ("Matthew, the gift of God"), and enthusiastically invited some of his "sinner" friends to meet the Lord Jesus. These were Jewish people like himself who did not follow the law or appear to have much interest in religious things. They were exactly the kind of people Jesus wanted to reach.

—*Be Diligent*, pages 34–35

6. Review Mark 2:13–22. Why did Jesus reach out to the outcasts of Jewish society? Why not the leaders? What did this reveal about His mission on earth? How did it stir up trouble in Jewish society?

From the Commentary

Matthew's friends were *patients* who needed a physician, and Jesus was that Physician. We have already seen that sin may be compared to sickness and forgiveness to having your health restored. Now we see that our Savior may be compared to a physician: He comes to us in our need; He makes a perfect diagnosis; He provides a final and complete cure; and *He pays the bill!* What a physician!

—*Be Diligent*, page 35

7. Are there some patients Jesus can't (or won't) heal? Explain. (Also, see Luke 19:10.) Why is admitting our sinfulness critical to salvation? Why wouldn't Jesus just heal all who are sinners? How does self-righteousness get in the way of forgiveness?

From the Commentary

While the first question the people asked had to do with the kind of company Jesus was keeping, their second question raised the issue of why Jesus was having such a good time with these people at the table. His conduct, to them, seemed inappropriate. John the Baptist was an austere man, somewhat of a recluse, but Jesus accepted invitations to meals, played with the children, and enjoyed social gatherings (Matt. 11:16–19). No doubt John's disciples were a bit scandalized to see Jesus at a party, and the pious disciples of the Pharisees (see Matt. 23:15) were quick to join them in their perplexity.

Jesus had already made it clear that He came to convert the sinners, not to compliment the self-righteous. Now He told them that He had come to bring gladness, not sadness. Thanks to the legalism imposed by the scribes and Pharisees, the Jewish religion had become a burden-some thing. The poor people were weighed down by rules and regulations that were impossible to obey (Matt. 23:4). "Life is not supposed to be a funeral!" Jesus told them. "God wants life to be a wedding feast! I am the Bridegroom and these people are my wedding guests. Are not wedding guests supposed to have a good time?"

—*Be Diligent*, page 36

8. Why do you think the religious leaders were upset with Jesus' focus on enjoying the company of the outcasts? Why was "fun" frowned upon? What does this entire passage tell us about how we ought to live out our faith today?

More to Consider: The Jews knew that marriage was one of the pictures used in the Old Testament to help explain Israel's relationship to the Lord. (See Isa. 54:5; Jer. 31:32.) How was their turn to foreign gods a kind of "spiritual adultery"? Read or skim through the book of Hosea. How does this book line up with Jesus' message as revealed in Mark?

From the Commentary

Jesus taught two important lessons about His ministry in Mark 2:21–22: (1) He came to save sinners, not to call the religious; and (2) He came to bring gladness and not sadness. The third lesson is this: He came to introduce the new, not to patch up the old.

The religious leaders were impressed with our Lord's teaching, and perhaps they would have been happy to make some of His ideas a part of their own religious tradition. They were hoping for some kind of compromise that would retain the best of pharisaic Judaism and the best of what Christ had to offer. But Jesus exposed the folly of that approach. It would be like tearing patches from a new unshrunk garment and sewing them on an old garment. You would ruin the new garment, and when the old garment was washed, the patches would shrink, rip away, and ruin that garment too (note Luke 5:36–39). Or, it would be like putting new unfermented wine in old brittle wineskins. As soon as the wine began to ferment

and the gases formed, the old skins would burst—and
you would lose both the wine and the skins.

—*Be Diligent*, pages 37–38

9. Why would the religious leaders of the time have been hoping Jesus
came to unite with the old teachings? What were some of the ways Jesus
surprised the religious leaders? Why weren't they more willing to accept
new teaching? How is this similar to the way churches deal with change
today?

From the Commentary

The Sabbath was cherished by the Jews as a sacred institu-
tion. God gave the people of Israel the Sabbath after they
came out of Egypt (Ex. 20:8–11; Neh. 9:14), and it was
a special sign between Israel and Jehovah (Ex. 31:13–17).
There is no record in Scripture that God ever gave the
Sabbath to any other nation. So, when Jesus began openly
to violate the Sabbath traditions, it was like declaring war
against the religious establishment. He began His cam-
paign by healing a man who had been sick for thirty-eight

years (John 5), and then followed with the events recorded in Mark 2:23—3:12.

Jewish tradition stated that there were thirty-nine acts that were strictly forbidden on the Sabbath. Moses had prohibited work on the Sabbath, but he did not give many specifics (Ex. 20:10). It was wrong to kindle a fire for cooking (Ex. 35:3), gather fuel (Num. 15:32ff.), carry burdens (Jer. 17:21ff.), or transact business (Neh. 10:31; 13:15, 19). But Jewish tradition went into great detail and even informed the people how far they could travel on the Sabbath (two hundred cubits, based on Josh. 3:4). In short, the Sabbath day had become a crushing burden, a symbol of the galling religious bondage that had captured the nation.

—Be Diligent, page 39

10. What was Jesus' next act of "Sabbath defiance" after the healing at the pool of Bethesda? What arguments did He give to defend His disciples? (See Matt. 12:3–4, 5–6, and 7–8.)

Looking Inward

Take a moment to reflect on all that you've explored thus far in this study of Mark 2:1—3:12. Review your notes and answers and think about how each of these things matters in your life today.

Tips for Small Groups: To get the most out of this section, form pairs or trios and have group members take turns answering these questions. Be honest and as open as you can in this discussion, but most of all, be encouraging and supportive of others. Be sensitive to those who are going through particularly difficult times and don't press for people to speak if they're uncomfortable doing so.

11. Who are the people you associate with most: people who think like you, or people who think differently? Which group do you think Jesus would want to spend the most time with? What are some ways you can relate to the outcasts Jesus hung out with? What are some ways you can relate to the religious leaders of today?

12. Jesus taught by example that we ought to enjoy the life God has given us. What are some ways you enjoy your God-given life? What's the difference between enjoying life as God gives it and enjoying life apart

from God? Why do so many people have a hard time being happy in their faith lives? What would Jesus say to those people?

13. How well do you deal with change? What are some of the ways Jesus has challenged you to grow and rethink things? What has made that easy for you? Difficult? What role does simple trust play in this aspect of your faith story?

Going Forward

14. Think of one or two things that you have learned that you'd like to work on in the coming week. Remember that this is all about quality, not quantity. It's better to work on one specific area of life and do it well than to work on many and do poorly (or to be so overwhelmed that you simply don't try).

Do you want to reach out more to people who aren't like you? Be specific. Go back through Mark 2:1—3:12 and put a star next to the phrase or verse that is most encouraging to you. Consider memorizing this verse.

Real-Life Application Ideas: Jesus riled up the religious leaders of His time by enjoying community with people who were considered outcasts. Think of some practical ways you can reach out to the fragmented people in your community. Could you help coordinate dinners for homeless folks? Organize and lead a weekly or monthly service for people who generally don't attend church—something that welcomes people of all walks and beliefs, a chance to enjoy community and a meal together, but without the traditional church trappings? How could such an event help people come to know Jesus? Look for ways to engage with people who think differently from you.

Seeking Help

15. Write a prayer below (or simply pray one in silence), inviting God to work on your mind and heart in those areas you've noted in the Going Forward section. Be honest about your desires and fears.

Notes for Small Groups:

- *Look for ways to put into practice the things you wrote in the Going Forward section. Talk with other group members about your ideas and commit to being accountable to one another.*

- *During the coming week, ask the Holy Spirit to continue to reveal truth to you from what you've read and studied.*

- *Before you start the next lesson, read Mark 3:13— 5:43. For more in-depth lesson preparation, read chapters 3 and 4, "The Servant, the Crowds, and the Kingdom" and "The Servant Conquers!," in* Be Diligent.

The Crowds and the Kingdom
(MARK 3:13—5:43)

Before you begin ...
- *Pray for the Holy Spirit to reveal truth and wisdom as you go through this lesson.*
- *Read Mark 3:13—5:43. This lesson references chapters 3 and 4 in* Be Diligent. *It will be helpful for you to have your Bible and a copy of the commentary available as you work through this lesson.*

Getting Started

From the Commentary

No matter where He went, God's Servant was thronged by excited crowds (Mark 3:7–9, 20, 32; 4:1). In Mark 3:13—4:34, we see our Lord's three responses to the pressure of the crowd.

In Jesus' first response (Mark 3:13–19), we consider the new nation He founded. The number of the disciples is significant because there were twelve tribes in the nation of Israel. In Genesis, God started with Jacob's twelve sons, and in Exodus, He built them into a mighty nation. Israel was chosen to bring the Messiah into the world so that through Him all the nations of the earth could be blessed (Gen. 12:1–3). However, the nation of Israel was now spiritually decayed and ready to reject her own Messiah.

—*Be Diligent*, page 45

1. Why did God have to establish a new holy nation (as Peter called the church in 1 Peter 2:9)? In what ways were the twelve apostles the nucleus of the new nation Jesus was establishing? (See Matt. 21:43.)

More to Consider: In the New Testament, you will find three other lists of the disciples' names: Matthew 10:2–4; Luke 6:14–16; and Acts 1:13. What do these lists teach us about Jesus' disciples? In the Matthew passage, the names are arranged in pairs: Peter and Andrew; James and John; Philip and Bartholomew; Thomas and Matthew; James, the son of Alphaeus, and Thaddaeus; Simon the Zealot and Judas Iscariot. Why might this arrangement be notable? (See Mark 6:7.)

2. Choose one verse or phrase from Mark 3:13—5:43 that stands out to you. This could be something you're intrigued by, something that makes you uncomfortable, something that puzzles you, something that resonates with you, or just something you want to examine further. Write that here.

Going Deeper

From the Commentary

> Our Lord's friends were sure that Jesus was confused, and possibly deranged! The great crowds they saw following Him, and the amazing reports they heard about Him, convinced them that He desperately needed help. He simply was not living a normal life, so His friends came to Capernaum to "take charge of him." Then his mother and "brethren" (Mark 6:3) traveled thirty miles from Nazareth to plead with Him to come home and get some rest, but even they were unable to get near Him. This is the only place in the gospel of Mark where Mary is seen, and her venture was a failure.
>
> —*Be Diligent*, page 47

3. Review Mark 3:20–21, 31–35. Was Jesus being rude to His family when He remained in the house? Explain. In what ways were their motives good? What would have been the result of yielding to His family's wishes? How did this play into the hands of the opposition?

From the Commentary

The crowds hoped that Jesus would deliver the nation and defeat Rome. Instead, He called twelve ordinary men and founded a "new nation," a spiritual nation whose citizens had their names written down in heaven (Luke 10:20; Phil. 3:20). The crowds wanted Jesus to behave like a loyal Jew and honor His family, but Jesus established a "new family" made up of all those who trusted Him and did the will of God. The crowds also expected Him to restore the kingdom and bring back Israel's lost glory, but His response was to announce a new kingdom, a spiritual kingdom.

"Kingdom" is a key word in this section (Mark 3:24; 4:11, 26, 30). John the Baptist had announced that the arrival of the King was near, and he had warned the people to prepare to meet Him (Mark 1:1–8). Jesus took up John's message and preached the good news of the kingdom and the necessity for sinners to repent and believe (Mark 1:14–15).

—*Be Diligent*, page 49

4. Review Mark 3:22–30; 4:1–34. What kind of kingdom was Jesus ushering in? How was it different from what the religious leaders expected? How was this significant to the story God was writing in that moment of history? How is it significant to believers today?

From the Commentary

Jesus healed a demoniac who was both blind and mute (Matt. 12:22–24), and the scribes and Pharisees used this miracle as an opportunity to attack Him. The crowd was saying, "Perhaps this Man is indeed the Son of David, the Messiah." But the religious leaders said, "No, He is in league with Beelzebub! It is Satan's power that is at work in Him, not God's power."

"Beelzebub" (or "Beelzebul") is a name for the Devil, and it means "master of the house." Jesus picked up on this meaning and gave a parable about a strong man guarding his house. To plunder the house, one must first overcome the strong man.

Jesus exposed both their bad theology and their faulty logic. If it was by the power of Satan that He had cast out the demon, then Satan was actually fighting against himself! This meant that Satan's house and kingdom were divided and therefore on the verge of collapse. Satan had been guarding that man carefully because the Devil does not want to lose any of his territory. The fact that Jesus delivered the man was proof that He was stronger than Satan and that Satan could not stop Him.

—Be Diligent, page 51

5. How did Jesus go on to explain the seriousness of the Pharisees' false accusation? What made the accusation serious? How might Jesus' response have affected the way the Pharisees viewed Him?

From the Commentary

In the parable of the lamp (Mark 4:21–25), our Lord used a common object (a lamp) in a familiar scene (a home). The lamp was a clay dish filled with oil, with a wick put into the oil. In order to give light, the lamp had to "use itself up," and the oil had to be replenished. If the lamp was not lit, or if it was covered up, it did the home no good.

—*Be Diligent*, page 54

6. In what ways were the apostles like the lamp in the parable? (See Mark 4:21–25.) Why is it important to take note of both *what* we hear (Mark 4:24) and *how* we hear (Luke 8:18)?

From the Commentary

Jesus had been teaching His disciples the Word, and now, in Mark 4:35–41, He would give them a practical test to see how much they had really learned. After all, the hearing of God's Word is intended to produce faith

(Rom. 10:17), and faith must always be tested. It is not enough for us merely to learn a lesson or be able to repeat a teaching. We must also be able to practice that lesson by faith, and that is one reason why God permits trials to come to our lives.

Did Jesus know that the storm was coming? Of course He did! The storm was a part of that day's curriculum. It would help the disciples understand a lesson that they did not even know they needed to learn: Jesus can be trusted in the storms of life. Many people have the idea that storms come to their lives only when they have disobeyed God, but this is not always the case.

—Be Diligent, pages 59–60

7. Review Mark 4:35–41. How did this storm reveal God's truth? What are other examples of storms in Scripture that revealed something about God to His people? How did the storm reinforce the message Jesus was teaching His disciples?

From the Commentary

> When Jesus and the disciples landed on the other side, they
> encountered two demoniacs, one of whom was especially
> vocal (see Matt. 8:28). This entire scene seems very unreal
> to us who live in so-called "modern civilization," but it
> would not be unreal in many mission fields. In fact, some
> Bible teachers believe that demon possession is becoming
> even more prevalent in today's "modern society."
>
> —*Be Diligent*, page 61

8. Review Mark 5:1–20. Why do you think the local people wanted Jesus
to go away, even after He had displayed power over demonic evil? Where
is such evil at work in our world today? How do various kinds of people
respond to it? How should we respond?

More to Consider: Why is it important never to underestimate the power of Satan? (See 1 Peter 5:8–9; Eph. 2:1–3.) Though the two men in the Gerasene graveyard were extreme examples of what Satan can do to people, what can they teach us about the destructive power of Satan?

From the Commentary

One crowd sighed with relief as they saw Jesus leave, but another crowd was waiting to welcome Him when He returned home to Capernaum. In that latter crowd stood two people who were especially anxious to see Him— Jairus, a man with a dying daughter; and an anonymous woman suffering from an incurable disease. It was Jairus who approached Jesus first, but it was the woman who was first helped, so we shall begin with her.

The contrast between these two needy people is striking and reveals the wideness of Christ's love and mercy. Jairus was an important synagogue officer, and the woman was an anonymous "nobody," yet Jesus welcomed and helped both of them. Jairus was about to lose a daughter who had given him twelve years of happiness (Mark 5:42), and the woman was about to lose an affliction that had brought her twelve years of sorrow. Being a synagogue officer, Jairus was no doubt wealthy, but his wealth could not save his dying daughter. The woman was already bankrupt! She had given the doctors all of her money, and yet none of them could cure her. Both Jairus and the poor woman found the answers to their needs at the feet of Jesus (Mark 5:22, 33).

The woman had a hemorrhage that was apparently incurable and was slowly destroying her. One can only imagine the pain and emotional pressure that sapped her strength day after day. When you consider her many disappointments with the doctors and the poverty it brought her, you wonder how she endured as long as she did. But there was one added burden: According to the law, she was ceremonially unclean, which greatly restricted both her religious and her social life (Lev. 15:19ff.). What a burden she carried!

However, she let nothing stand in her way as she pushed through the crowd and came to Jesus. She could have used any number of excuses to convince herself to stay away from Him. She might have said, "I'm not important enough to ask Jesus for help!" or "Look, He's going with Jairus, so I won't bother Him now." She could have argued that nothing else had helped her, so why try again? Or she might have concluded that it was not right to come to Jesus as a last resort, after visiting all those physicians. However, she laid aside all arguments and excuses and came by faith to Jesus.

—*Be Diligent*, pages 65–66

9. Review Mark 5:21–34. What does this passage reveal about the kinds of people who need Jesus? How did Jesus respond to the people in this passage? What message is there in this story for our churches today?

From the Commentary

> It was not easy for Jairus to come to Jesus publicly and ask
> for His help. The religious leaders who were opposed to
> Jesus would certainly not approve, nor would some of the
> other synagogue leaders. The things that Jesus had done
> and taught in the synagogues had aroused the anger of
> the scribes and Pharisees, some of whom were probably
> Jairus's friends. But Jairus was desperate, as many people
> are when they come to Jesus. He would rather lose his
> friends and save his beloved daughter.
>
> —*Be Diligent*, page 68

10. Review Mark 5:35–43. Consider the three statements Jesus made in verses 36, 39, and 41. What do these statements teach us about Jesus? How did Jesus lead Jairus to victory?

Looking Inward

Take a moment to reflect on all that you've explored thus far in this study of Mark 3:13—5:43. Review your notes and answers and think about how each of these things matters in your life today.

Tips for Small Groups: To get the most out of this section, form pairs or trios and have group members take turns answering these questions. Be honest and as open as you can in this discussion, but most of all, be encouraging and supportive of others. Be sensitive to those who are going through particularly difficult times and don't press for people to speak if they're uncomfortable doing so.

11. Jesus' family didn't understand Him. What are some ways your family doesn't understand your life? How does your family respond to your faith? If they don't believe as you do, how do you handle that? Have you ever chosen faith over family? If so, what has that involved?

12. What are some of the storms you've faced in life? Where was God in those storms? What did He teach you through them?

13. Are you the sort of person who would push through the crowds to reach Jesus? Or are you someone who would hang back, hoping He might see you? What does this tell you about how you live out your faith? What would give you the confidence to approach Jesus in your faith life today?

Going Forward

14. Think of one or two things that you have learned that you'd like to work on in the coming week. Remember that this is all about quality, not quantity. It's better to work on one specific area of life and do it well than to work on many and do poorly (or to be so overwhelmed that you simply don't try).

Do you want to learn how to trust Jesus better during the storms in your life? Be specific. Go back through Mark 3:13—5:43 and put a star next to the phrase or verse that is most encouraging to you. Consider memorizing this verse.

Real-Life Application Ideas: If you have family members who don't agree with your faith choices (or understand them), make it a point this week to reach out to those family members in love. Don't try to convince them to believe what you do, but share with them why you believe what you do, assuring them as well that you love them no matter where they are in their journey today.

Seeking Help

15. Write a prayer below (or simply pray one in silence), inviting God to work on your mind and heart in those areas you've noted in the Going Forward section. Be honest about your desires and fears.

Notes for Small Groups:

- *Look for ways to put into practice the things you wrote in the Going Forward section. Talk with other group members about your ideas and commit to being accountable to one another.*

- *During the coming week, ask the Holy Spirit to continue to reveal truth to you from what you've read and studied.*

- *Before you start the next lesson, read Mark 6. For more in-depth lesson preparation, read chapter 5, "Will Anyone Trust God's Servant?," in* Be Diligent.

Unbelief
(MARK 6)

Before you begin ...
- *Pray for the Holy Spirit to reveal truth and wisdom as you go through this lesson.*
- *Read Mark 6. This lesson references chapter 5 in* Be Diligent. *It will be helpful for you to have your Bible and a copy of the commentary available as you work through this lesson.*

Getting Started

From the Commentary

Charles Darwin said that *belief* was "the most complete of all distinctions between man and the lower animals." If this observation is true, it suggests that lack of faith on man's part puts him on the same level as the animals! Agnostic orator Col. Robert Ingersoll took a different point of view, for he once described a believer as "a songless bird in a cage." You would probably agree that his words better describe an *un*believer!

One of the central themes in chapter 6 of Mark's gospel is the unbelief of people who came into contact with God's Servant. All of these people had every reason to trust Jesus Christ, yet all of them failed to do so, including His own disciples!

—*Be Diligent*, page 73

1. Where do you see unbelief at work in Mark 6? In what ways does God take unbelief seriously? (See Heb. 3:12.) Why is this important to understand?

2. Choose one verse or phrase from Mark 6 that stands out to you. This could be something you're intrigued by, something that makes you uncomfortable, something that puzzles you, something that resonates with you, or just something you want to examine further. Write that here.

Going Deeper

From the Commentary

Jesus returned to Nazareth, where a year before He had been rejected by the people and evicted from the synagogue (Luke 4:16–30). It was certainly an act of grace on His part to give the people another opportunity to hear His Word, believe, and be saved, and yet their hearts were still hard. This time, they did not evict Him: they simply did not take Him seriously.

Our Lord's reputation had once again preceded Him, so He was permitted to teach in the synagogue. Keep in mind that He was ministering to people who knew Him well, because Nazareth was His "hometown." However, these acquaintances had no spiritual perception at all. In fact, Jesus reminded them of what He had told them at that first dramatic visit, that a prophet is without honor in his own country and among his own people (Mark 6:4; Luke 4:24; John 4:44).

Two things astonished these people: His mighty works and His wonderful wisdom. Actually, Jesus did not do any mighty works while He was there, so the people must have been referring to the reports they had heard about His miracles (see Mark 1:28, 45; 3:7–8; 5:20–21).

—*Be Diligent*, pages 73–74

3. Review Mark 6:1–6. What was the reason for these people's unbelief? What was the reputation that preceded Jesus? How did their unbelief hinder Jesus' ministry? How is this true in the church today?

More to Consider: "Familiarity breeds contempt" is a well-known maxim that goes all the way back to Publius the Syrian, who lived in 2 BC. Aesop wrote a fable to illustrate it. In Aesop's fable, a fox had never before seen a lion, and when he first met the king of the beasts, the fox was nearly frightened to death. At their second meeting, the fox was not frightened quite as much; and the third time he met the lion, the fox went up and chatted with him! "And so it is," Aesop concluded, "that familiarity makes even the most frightening things seem quite harmless." How is this evident in Jesus' story in Mark 6? How is this true in churches today?

From the Commentary

The people of Nazareth were "offended at him," which literally means "they stumbled over him." The Greek word gives us our English word *scandalize*. Kenneth Wuest wrote in his book *Wuest's Word Studies* (Eerdmans), "They could not explain Him, so they rejected Him." Jesus was certainly a "stone of stumbling" to them because of their unbelief (Isa. 8:14; Rom. 9:32–33; 1 Peter 2:8).

Twice in the gospel record you find Jesus marveling. As this passage reveals, He marveled at the unbelief of the Jews, and He marveled at the great faith of a Roman centurion, a Gentile (Luke 7:9).

—Be Diligent, page 75

4. Why would the people reject Jesus simply because they didn't understand Him? How does our lack of understanding contribute to poor decisions in faith and life? What does this teach us about seeking true understanding before coming to conclusions?

From Today's World

In the past, people often took things at face value; they didn't question. Or they embraced the idea that something could be a mystery without the need to explain it away. But in the modern age, where information about nearly everything is just a few keystrokes away, everything is put to the test. While the reliability of information on the Internet ranges from "certain" to "unbelievable," it's still the go-to place for people in search of proofs and evidence. Our modern society wants solid evidence before we believe anything. The demystification of technology has contributed to this desire for proof.

5. How has the information age contributed to people's doubt of God's truth? How has it helped people believe? Why is it so important for people to accept mystery in order to know Jesus? Where is mystery in our modern culture?

From the Commentary

When the Lord originally called the twelve apostles, His purpose was to teach and train them so that they might assist Him and eventually be able to take His place when He returned to the Father (Mark 3:13–15). Before sending them out, He reaffirmed their authority to heal and to cast out demons (Mark 6:7), and He gave them some pointed instructions (see Matt. 10 for a more detailed account of this sermon).

He told them to take what they already owned and not go out and buy special equipment for their itinerant travels.

They were not to be loaded down with extra baggage. (You cannot miss the note of urgency in this "commissioning sermon.") Jesus wanted them to be adequately supplied, but not to the point of ceasing to live by faith. The word *bag* means "a beggar's bag." They were definitely not to beg for either food or money.

As they ministered from place to place, they would encounter both hospitality and hostility, both friends and enemies. He cautioned them to stay at one house in each community and not to "pick and choose" when it came to their food and accommodations. After all, they were there to be profitable servants, not pampered guests. If a house or a village did not receive them, they had His permission to declare God's judgment on those people.

—*Be Diligent*, page 76

6. Review Mark 6:7–13. Why was it so important that the disciples not overprepare for their trips? What kinds of reactions did they have as they went from place to place? It was customary for Jews to shake the dust off their feet when leaving Gentile territory. How would this practice have been received if they shook off the dust after leaving their fellow Jews? (See Luke 10:10–11; Acts 13:51.)

From the Commentary

> We noted before (Mark 3:16–19) that a comparison of
> the lists of the apostles' names reveals that the names
> are given in several pairs: Peter and Andrew, James and
> John, Philip and Bartholomew, etc. Jesus sent them out
> in pairs because it is always easier and safer for servants
> to travel and work together. "Two are better than one"
> (Eccl. 4:9), and the law, as previously observed, required
> two witnesses to verify a matter (Deut. 17:6; 19:15; 2 Cor.
> 13:1). They would not only help each other; they would
> also learn from each other.
>
> The men went out and did what Jesus told them to do. It
> is remarkable that a band of ordinary men could go out in
> this way to represent Almighty God, and that they could
> demonstrate their authority by performing miracles.
>
> —*Be Diligent*, page 77

7. What did the disciples proclaim when they went out to minister? (See
Mark 6:12–13; Luke 9:6.) What does the fact that these were ordinary
men teach us about how God accomplishes His purposes? What does this
teach us for today?

From the Commentary

It is remarkable that there is no evidence that any of the Jewish leaders did anything to rescue John the Baptist after he had been arrested. The common people considered John a prophet sent from God, but the religious leaders did not obey John's message (Mark 11:27–33). John's death was the first of three notable violent deaths in the history of Israel. The other two are the crucifixion of Christ and the stoning of Stephen (Acts 7). For the significance of these events, review the comments on Mark 3:22–30. Herod had feared that John's messages would stir up a revolt among the people, something he wanted to avoid. Also, he wanted to please his wife, even though it meant the murdering of a godly man.

John's disciples were permitted to take the body of their leader and bury it, and then they went to tell Jesus what had happened (Matt. 14:12). No doubt the report of John's death deeply stirred our Lord, for He knew that one day His own life would be laid down.

—*Be Diligent*, pages 78–79

8. Why was John the Baptist essentially left to die after he'd been arrested? What does this say about the political climate of the time? What does it tell us about John's supporters? About Jesus Himself?

More to Consider: In addition to the story of John the Baptist's death,
we meet Herod Antipas one more time in the Gospels: when he "tried"
Jesus and hoped to see the Lord perform a miracle (Luke 23:6–12).
What was Jesus' response to this man? Read Luke 13:31–35. Why do
you think Jesus used this particular description?

From the Commentary

Jesus took His disciples to a secluded place so that they
might rest after their labors. He wanted to discuss their
ministry with them and prepare them for their next mission. As Vance Havner has said, "If you don't come apart
and rest, you will come apart." Even God's Servant-Son
needed time to rest, fellowship with His friends, and find
renewal from the Father.

Another factor was the growing opposition of both the
political and the religious leaders. Herod's murder of John
the Baptist was evidence enough that the "climate" was
now changing and that Jesus and His disciples had to
be careful. In the next chapter, we shall encounter the
hostility of the Jewish religious leaders, and, of course, the
political enthusiasm of the crowds was always a problem
(John 6:15ff.). The best thing to do was to get away.

But the overzealous crowds would not leave Him alone.
They followed Him to the area near Bethsaida, hoping to
see Him perform some miraculous cures (Luke 9:10–11;
John 6:1ff.). In spite of the interruption to His plans, the

Lord welcomed them, taught them the Word, and healed those who were afflicted.

—*Be Diligent*, pages 79–80

9. Review Mark 6:30–56. How did Jesus deal with interruptions? With lack of rest? With needy people? How do you think we today should deal with these things?

From the Commentary

Spiritual blessings must be balanced with burdens and battles, otherwise, we may become pampered children instead of mature sons and daughters. On a previous occasion, Jesus had led His disciples into a storm following an exciting day of teaching (Mark 4:35–41). Now, after a time of miraculous ministry, He again led them into a storm. In the book of Acts, it is interesting to note that the "storm" of official persecution began after the disciples had won five thousand people to Christ (Acts 4:1–4). Perhaps while they were in confinement, the apostles recalled the storm that followed the feeding of the five thousand, and they must have encouraged themselves with the assurance that Jesus would come to them and see them through.

In that first storm experience, the disciples had Jesus in the boat with them, but this time, He was on the mountain praying for them. He was teaching them to live by faith. (For that matter, even when He was in the ship with them, they were still afraid!) The scene illustrates the situation of God's people today: We are in the midst of this stormy world, toiling and seemingly ready to sink, but He is in glory interceding for us. When the hour seems the darkest, He will come to us—and we will reach shore!

—*Be Diligent*, page 82

10. How did the disciples' testing experiences grow their faith and courage? How does this happen for believers today?

Looking Inward

Take a moment to reflect on all that you've explored thus far in this study of Mark 6. Review your notes and answers and think about how each of these things matters in your life today.

Tips for Small Groups: To get the most out of this section, form pairs or trios and have group members take turns answering these questions. Be honest and as open as you can in this discussion, but most of all, be encouraging and supportive of others. Be sensitive to those who are going through particularly difficult times and don't press for people to speak if they're uncomfortable doing so.

11. When have you struggled with unbelief? What led to those struggles? How did you find your way through? In what ways were your struggles like or unlike what the disciples went through?

12. Have you ever rejected something simply because you didn't understand it? Has this ever been true in your faith life? Explain. Where can you go to find the ability to trust in things you can't understand?

13. How do you deal with lack of rest? With interruptions? What can Jesus' example teach you about both?

Going Forward

14. Think of one or two things that you have learned that you'd like to work on in the coming week. Remember that this is all about quality, not quantity. It's better to work on one specific area of life and do it well than to work on many and do poorly (or to be so overwhelmed that you simply don't try).

Do you want to learn how to be more trusting in times of testing? Be specific. Go back through Mark 6 and put a star next to the phrase or verse that is most encouraging to you. Consider memorizing this verse.

Real-Life Application Ideas: Jesus got away from the crowds (and sometimes His disciples too) to pray and rest. How well are you doing with these two important aspects of life? Talk with your family members, and come up with a time when you can go away for a day or so to simply relax in God's presence and pray. Don't bring along distractions; just embrace a time of true rest.

Seeking Help

15. Write a prayer below (or simply pray one in silence), inviting God to work on your mind and heart in those areas you've noted in the Going Forward section. Be honest about your desires and fears.

Notes for Small Groups:

- *Look for ways to put into practice the things you wrote in the Going Forward section. Talk with other group members about your ideas and commit to being accountable to one another.*

- *During the coming week, ask the Holy Spirit to continue to reveal truth to you from what you've read and studied.*

- *Before you start the next lesson, read Mark 7—9. For more in-depth lesson preparation, read chapters 6 and 7, "The Servant-Teacher" and "The Servant's Secrets," in* Be Diligent.

Teacher
(MARK 7—9)

Before you begin …

- *Pray for the Holy Spirit to reveal truth and wisdom as you go through this lesson.*
- *Read Mark 7—9. This lesson references chapters 6 and 7 in* Be Diligent. *It will be helpful for you to have your Bible and a copy of the commentary available as you work through this lesson.*

Getting Started

From the Commentary

We see in Mark 7:1—8:26 three ministries of Jesus, the Servant-Teacher.

The first ministry involved teaching the Jews (Mark 7:1–23). There are four stages in this drama, and the first is *accusation* (7:1–5). The Jewish religious leaders were now openly hostile toward the Lord and His ministry. It was not unusual for them to follow Him from place to place simply to watch for something to criticize. In this case, they accused the disciples of failing to practice the Jewish ceremonial washing. These washings had nothing to do with personal hygiene, nor were they commanded in the law. They were a part of the tradition that the scribes and Pharisees had given to the people to add to their burdens (Matt. 23:4).

Our Lord had already violated their Sabbath traditions (Mark 2:23—3:5), so the Jews were eager to accuse Him when they saw the disciples eat "with defiled hands."

—*Be Diligent*, page 87

1. Why would such a seemingly trivial matter upset these religious leaders? Why would they feel compelled to defend their ceremonial washings?

More to Consider: Whenever the Jews practiced these washings, they declared that they were special and that other people were unclean. They believed that when they went to the marketplace to buy food, they could possibly be "defiled" by a Gentile or a Samaritan. How is this an example of a good habit or ritual going bad? What are some other examples of this in history and in the modern church?

2. Choose one verse or phrase from Mark 7—9 that stands out to you. This could be something you're intrigued by, something that makes you uncomfortable, something that puzzles you, something that resonates with you, or just something you want to examine further. Write that here.

Going Deeper

From the Commentary

> In defending their tradition, the Pharisees eroded their own characters and also the character of the Word of God. They were hypocrites, "playactors" whose religious worship was practiced in vain. True worship must come from the heart, and it must be directed by God's truth, not man's personal ideas. What a tragedy that religious

people would ignorantly practice their religion and become the worse for doing it!

But they were not only destroying their character; they were also destroying the influence and authority of the very Word of God that they claimed to be defending. Note the tragic sequence: teaching their doctrines as God's Word (Mark 7:7); laying aside God's Word (Mark 7:8); rejecting God's Word (Mark 7:9); finally, robbing God's Word of its power (Mark 7:13). People who revere man-made traditions above the Word of God eventually lose the power of God's Word in their lives. No matter how devout they may appear, their hearts are far from God.

—*Be Diligent*, page 89

3. How were the Jewish religious leaders honoring their traditions above God's Word? What are some ways believers and leaders do this in today's church?

From the Commentary

The human heart is sinful and produces all manner of evil desires, thoughts, and actions, everything from murder to envy ("an evil eye"). Jesus had no illusions about human nature, as do some liberal theologians and humanistic teachers today. He realized that man is a sinner, unable to control or change his own nature, *and that is why Jesus came to earth—to die for lost sinners.*

The Jewish dietary laws were given by God to teach His chosen people to make a difference between what was clean and what was unclean. (No doubt there were also some practical reasons involved, such as sanitation and health.) To disobey these laws was a matter of ceremonial defilement, and that was an external matter. Food *ends up* in the stomach, but sin *begins* in the heart. The food we eat is digested and the waste evacuated, but sin remains and it produces defilement and death.

—*Be Diligent*, page 91

4. Contrast human traditions with God's truth. Why did Jesus' words challenging traditions irritate the Jewish religious leaders? Why would this make them want to silence Jesus? How did this increased opposition affect Jesus' presence in the crowded areas?

From the Commentary

The second ministry that showed Jesus as the Servant-Teacher involved helping the Gentiles (Mark 7:24—8:9).

Of the thirty-five recorded miracles in the Gospels, four directly involve women: the healing of Peter's mother-in-law (Mark 1:30–31); the raising of the widow's son (Luke 7:11–17); the raising of Lazarus (John 11); and the casting out of the demon as recorded in Mark 7:24–30.

Jesus came to this area (about forty miles from Capernaum) so that He might have some privacy, but a concerned mother discovered He was there and came to Him for help. There were many obstacles in her way, yet she overcame them all by faith and got what she needed.

—*Be Diligent*, page 92

5. How did this mother's faith ultimately help her and her daughter to triumph? What message is there in this story about the persistence of faith?

From the Commentary

The region of Decapolis ("ten cities") was also Gentile territory, but before Jesus left the region, the people were glorifying the God of Israel (Matt. 15:30–31). The man they brought to Jesus was handicapped both by deafness and an impediment in his speech, and Jesus healed him.

Since the man was deaf, he could not hear our Lord's words, but he could feel Jesus' fingers in his ear and the touch on his tongue, and this would encourage the man's faith. The "sigh" was an inward groan, our Lord's compassionate response to the pain and sorrow sin has brought into the world. It was also a prayer to the Father on behalf of the handicapped man. (The same word is used in connection with prayer in Rom. 8:23, and the noun in Rom. 8:26.)

—*Be Diligent*, pages 93–94

6. Review Mark 7:31–37. Why do you think Jesus told the people not to tell anyone about His healing of the deaf man? Why do you think Jesus healed this man in a secluded place? This miracle is recorded only in Mark's gospel. Why might hearing about this Gentile's healing have been particularly valuable for Mark's Roman readers?

From the Commentary

The third ministry that showed Jesus as the Servant-Teacher involved warning the disciples (Mark 8:10–26).

Jesus and the disciples crossed to the western side of the Sea of Galilee where they were met by the Pharisees who were still angry at Him because of His earlier indictment of their hypocrisy (Mark 7:1–23). This time they tempted Him to prove His divine authority by giving them a sign from heaven. They did not want an earthly miracle, such as the healing of a sick person. They wanted Him to do something spectacular, like bring fire from heaven or bread from heaven (John 6:30–31). This would prove He was indeed sent from God.

Our Lord's response was one of deep grief and disappointment (see Mark 7:34; 8:12). How tragic that the religious leaders of God's chosen people should be so hardhearted and spiritually blind! Their desire for a sign from heaven was but another evidence of their unbelief, for faith does not ask for signs. True faith takes God at His Word and is satisfied with the inward witness of the Spirit.

—*Be Diligent*, page 95

7. Review Mark 8:10–13. The Pharisees seemed to have been following Jesus wherever He went. Why did they do this? Why couldn't they just leave Him alone? Why did they ask for a big sign? What was their hope?

From the Commentary

If you were to go around asking your friends, "What do people say about me?" they would take it as an evidence of pride. What difference does it really make what people think or say about us? We are not that important! But what people believe and say about Jesus Christ *is* important, for He is the Son of God and the only Savior of sinners.

Your confession concerning Jesus Christ is a matter of life or death (John 8:21, 24; 1 John 2:22–27; 4:1–3). The citizens of Caesarea Philippi would say, "Caesar is lord!" That confession might identify them as loyal Roman citizens, but it could never save them from their sins and from eternal hell. The only confession that saves us is "Jesus is Lord!" (1 Cor. 12:1–3) when it comes from a heart that truly believes in Him (Rom. 10:9–10).

It is remarkable the number of different opinions the people held about Jesus, though the same situation probably exists today. That some thought He was John the Baptist is especially perplexing, since John and Jesus had been seen publicly together. They were quite different in personality and ministry (Matt. 11:16–19), so it seems strange that the people would confuse them.

—*Be Diligent*, pages 101–2

8. Why was it so important for Jesus to ask what the people were saying about Him? What did this teach the disciples? Why might some people

have mistaken Jesus for John the Baptist? What does this reveal about their hopes? Fears?

From the Commentary

> Now that they had confessed their faith in Christ (but see John 6:66–71), the disciples were ready for the "secret" Jesus wanted to share with them: He was going with them to Jerusalem, where He would die on a cross. From this point on, Mark will focus on their journey to Jerusalem, and the emphasis will be on Jesus' approaching death and resurrection (Mark 9:30–32; 10:32–34).
>
> This announcement stunned the disciples. If He is indeed the Christ of God, as they had confessed, then why would He be rejected by the religious leaders? Why would these leaders crucify Him? Did not the Old Testament Scriptures promise that the Messiah would defeat all their enemies and establish a glorious kingdom for Israel? There was something wrong somewhere and the disciples were confused.
>
> —*Be Diligent*, page 103

9. Review Mark 8:31–38. Why do you think Jesus waited so long to reveal this secret? What sort of welcome did the disciples expect in Jerusalem? How might this secret have affected their confidence? Why is it appropriate that Peter was the one to express his concern?

More to Consider: Peter's protest was born out of his ignorance of God's will and his deep love for his Lord. One minute Peter was a rock, and the next he was a stumbling block! Dr. G. Campbell Morgan said, "The man who loves Jesus, but who shuns God's method, is a stumbling block to Him." Peter did not yet understand the relationship between suffering and glory. Read 1 Peter 1:6–8; 4:13—5:10. How do these passages reveal the truth that Peter learned from his errors?

From the Commentary

The Christian life is "a land of hills and valleys" (Deut. 11:11). In one day, a disciple can move from the glory of heaven to the attacks of hell. When our Lord and His three friends returned to the other nine disciples, they found them involved in a dual problem: They were unable to deliver a boy from demonic control, and the scribes were debating with them and perhaps even taunting them because of their failure. As always, it was Jesus who stepped in to solve the problem.

The boy was both deaf and mute (Mark 9:17, 25), and the demon was doing his best to destroy him. Imagine what it would be like for that father to try to care for the boy and protect him! Jesus had given His disciples authority to cast out demons (Mark 6:7, 13), and yet their ministry to the boy was ineffective.

—*Be Diligent*, pages 108–9

10. Why was the disciples' attempt to heal the boy ineffective? How might the timing of this event (soon after Jesus' had revealed to them His future death and resurrection) have affected the disciples' confidence? What does this teach us about trusting God even when facing uncertainty or fear?

Looking Inward

Take a moment to reflect on all that you've explored thus far in this study of Mark 7—9. Review your notes and answers and think about how each of these things matters in your life today.

Tips for Small Groups: To get the most out of this section, form pairs or trios and have group members take turns answering these questions. Be honest and as open as you can in this discussion, but most of all, be encouraging and supportive of others. Be sensitive to those who are going through particularly difficult times and don't press for people to speak if they're uncomfortable doing so.

11. What are some good old habits that you find difficult to let go of in light of what it means to be a follower of Christ? How do you determine whether something you're doing is a bad habit or a good discipline?

12. Have you ever insisted on tradition above God's will? Why are you sometimes tempted to give traditions more value than what God wants of you? Is it easier to trust tradition or trust God? Explain.

13. How is your faith affected when you question God's decisions in your life or the lives of loved ones? How can you learn to trust God in the midst of that uncertainty?

Going Forward

14. Think of one or two things that you have learned that you'd like to work on in the coming week. Remember that this is all about quality, not quantity. It's better to work on one specific area of life and do it well than to work on many and do poorly (or to be so overwhelmed that you simply don't try).

Do you want to learn how to trust God's will above even good traditions? Be specific. Go back through Mark 7—9 and put a star next to the phrase or verse that is most encouraging to you. Consider memorizing this verse.

Real-Life Application Ideas: Take inventory of the spiritual practices that you've been doing for a long time—everything from the way you pray (and how often) to the church you attend and everything in between. Then ask God for guidance to help you sort through these things. Examine whether these practices are truly growing your faith and bringing you closer to God, or if they are getting in the way of your relationship with Him. Then adjust your habits accordingly.

Seeking Help

15. Write a prayer below (or simply pray one in silence), inviting God to work on your mind and heart in those areas you've noted in the Going Forward section. Be honest about your desires and fears.

Notes for Small Groups:

- *Look for ways to put into practice the things you wrote in the Going Forward section. Talk with other group members about your ideas and commit to being accountable to one another.*

- *During the coming week, ask the Holy Spirit to continue to reveal truth to you from what you've read and studied.*

- *Before you start the next lesson, read Mark 10. For more in-depth lesson preparation, read chapter 8, "The Servant's Paradoxes," in* Be Diligent.

Paradoxes
(MARK 10)

Before you begin ...
- *Pray for the Holy Spirit to reveal truth and wisdom as you go through this lesson.*
- *Read Mark 10. This lesson references chapter 8 in* Be Diligent. *It will be helpful for you to have your Bible and a copy of the commentary available as you work through this lesson.*

Getting Started

From the Commentary

As a master Teacher, our Lord used many different approaches in sharing God's Word: symbols, miracles, types, parables, proverbs, and paradoxes. A paradox is a statement that seems to contradict itself and yet expresses a valid truth or principle. "When I am weak, then am I strong" is a paradox (2 Cor. 12:10; also see 2 Cor. 6:8–10). There are times when the best way to state a truth is by means of paradox, and this chapter describes our Lord doing just that. He could have preached long sermons, but instead, He gave us five important lessons that can be expressed in five succinct, paradoxical statements.

—*Be Diligent*, page 117

1. How can using paradoxes (seeming contradictions) be a great teaching method? Where do you see paradoxes in Mark 10?

2. Choose one verse or phrase from Mark 10 that stands out to you. This could be something you're intrigued by, something that makes you uncomfortable, something that puzzles you, something that resonates with you, or just something you want to examine further. Write that here.

Going Deeper

From the Commentary

Jesus completed His ministry in Galilee, left Capernaum, and came to the Trans-Jordan area, still on His way to the city of Jerusalem (Mark 10:32). This district was ruled by Herod Antipas, which may explain why the Pharisees tried to trap Him by asking a question about divorce. After all, John the Baptist had been slain because he preached against Herod's adulterous marriage (Mark 6:14–29).

But there was more than politics involved in their trick question, because divorce was a very controversial subject among the Jewish rabbis. No matter what answer Jesus gave, He would be sure to displease somebody, and this might give opportunity to arrest Him. The verbs indicate that the Pharisees "kept asking him," as though they hoped to provoke Him to say something incriminating.

In that day there were two conflicting views on divorce, and which view you espoused depended on how you interpreted the phrase "some uncleanness" in Deuteronomy 24:1–4. The followers of Rabbi Hillel were quite lenient in their interpretation and permitted a man to divorce his wife for any reason, even the burning of his food. But the school of Rabbi Shimmai was much more strict and taught that the critical words "some uncleanness" referred only to premarital sin. If a newly married husband discovered that his wife was not a virgin, then he could put her away.

—Be Diligent, pages 117–18

3. Review Mark 10:1–12. How did Jesus respond to the question about divorce? How did He redirect the debate? (See Deut. 24:1–4.) What were the risks of even answering this question (or any of the Pharisees' questions)?

More to Consider: As you study this passage, it is important to note two facts. First, it was the husband who divorced the wife, not the wife who divorced the husband. Second, the official "bill of divorcement" was given to the wife to declare her status and to assure any prospective husband that she was indeed free to remarry. Among the Jews, the question was not "May a divorced woman marry again?" because remarriage was permitted and even expected. The big question was "What are the legal grounds for a man to divorce his wife?" Why would this have been such an important question for the Jews? How was the way they looked at divorce similar to the way believers (and nonbelievers) consider it today? What would Jesus say to people today who argue about the legal grounds for divorce?

From the Commentary

> Mark 10:9 warns us that *man* cannot separate those who
> have been united in marriage, *but God can.* Since He
> established marriage, He has the right to lay down the
> rules. A divorce may be legal according to our laws and
> yet not be right in the eyes of God. He expects married
> people to practice commitment to each other (Mark 10:7)
> and to remain true to each other.
>
> —*Be Diligent*, page 120

4. How might God separate those who are united in marriage? Why do so
many people view divorce today as an "easy way out"? What does it mean
to take seriously our marriage vows to each other and to the Lord?

From Today's World

It's easy to point to the secular world and its divorce statistics and say, "See?
If only you knew Jesus, things wouldn't fall apart." But that would be inac-
curate. The divorce rate inside the church is just about the same as outside
of it. Part of this may be because of the relative ease of getting a divorce (in
some states it's easier than others). And with popular media making news

out of every famous person's divorce (whether actor or singer or politician), there's just no escaping the reality of statistics that suggest nearly half of all marriages end before death.

5. Why is divorce so rampant even among Christians? What has changed between the time of Jesus and today that might account for the high number of divorces? How might Jesus respond to the current state of marriage in our world?

From the Commentary

First marriage, then children; the sequence is logical. Unlike many "moderns" today, the Jews of that day looked on children as a blessing and not a burden, a rich treasure from God and not a liability (Ps. 127—128). To be without children brought a couple both sorrow and disgrace.

It was customary for parents to bring their children to the rabbis for a blessing, and so it was reasonable that they would bring the little ones to Jesus. Some were infants in arms (Luke 18:15), while others were young children able to walk, and He welcomed them all.

—*Be Diligent*, page 120

6. Why did the disciples rebuke the people and try to keep the children away from Jesus? (See also Matt. 15:23 for another instance of their hardness of heart.) What does this say about how they did or didn't value children? What lesson did they miss from Jesus' earlier teaching? (See Mark 9:36–37.)

From the Commentary

Of all the people who ever came to the feet of Jesus, the rich young ruler in Mark 10:17 is the only one who went away worse than he came. And yet he had so much in his favor! He was a young man (Matt. 19:22) with great potential. He was respected by others, for he held some ruling office, perhaps in a local court (Luke 18:18). Certainly he had manners and morals, and there was enough desire in his heart for spiritual things that he ran up to Jesus and bowed at His feet. In every way, he was an ideal young man, and when Jesus beheld him, He loved him.

With all of his fine qualities, the young man was very superficial in his views of spiritual things. He certainly had a shallow view of salvation, for he thought that he

could *do something* to earn or merit eternal life. This
was a common belief in that day among the Jews (John
6:28), and it is very common today. Most unsaved people
think that God will one day add up their good works and
their bad works, and if their good works exceed their bad
works, they will get into heaven.

—*Be Diligent*, pages 121–22

7. Review Mark 10:17–31. What makes the good-works approach to
salvation superficial? Why do you think the young man thought he could
settle his account with God by doing works? What did this reveal about
his heart?

From the Commentary

Our Lord's directions in Mark 10:21 are not to be applied
to everyone who wants to become a disciple, because Jesus
was addressing the specific needs of the rich young ruler.
The man was rich, so Jesus told him to liquidate his estate
and give the money to the poor. The man was a ruler, so
Jesus told him to take up a cross and follow Him, which

would be a humbling experience. Jesus offered this man the gift of eternal life, but he turned it down. It is difficult to receive a gift when your fist is clenched around money and the things money can buy. The Greek word translated "grieved" gives the picture of storm clouds gathering. The man walked out of the sunshine and into a storm! He wanted to get salvation on his terms, and he was disappointed.

—*Be Diligent*, page 123

8. Why were the disciples shocked at Jesus' declaration about wealth? How do the message in the book of Job and the example of Christ and the apostles in Mark 10 reveal the error in the Jews' thinking that wealth was evidence of God's blessing? Where do you find this wrong message still preached in today's church?

More to Consider: Peter's response indicated that there were a few problems in his own heart: "What then will there be for us?" (Matt. 19:27 NASB). How does this statement reveal a rather commercial view of the Christian life? Contrast Peter's words with those of the three Hebrew men in Daniel 3:16–18 and with Peter's later testimony in Acts 3:6.

From the Commentary

The destination was still Jerusalem, and Jesus was still leading the way. As Mark wrote his account of the Savior's journey to Calvary, he must have meditated much on the great "Servant Songs" in Isaiah 42—53. "For the Lord GOD will help me; therefore shall I not be confounded: therefore have I set my face like a flint, and I know that I shall not be ashamed" (Isa. 50:7). We cannot but admire the courage of God's Servant as He made His way to Calvary, and we should adore Him all the more because He did it for us.

We must try to understand the bewilderment and fear of His followers, for this was a difficult experience for them and not at all what they had planned or expected. Each new announcement of His death only added to their perplexity. In the first two announcements (Mark 8:31; 9:31), Jesus had told them *what* would occur, but now He told them *where* His passion will take place—in the Holy City of Jerusalem! In this third announcement (Mark 10:32–34), He also included the part that the Gentiles would play in His trial and death, and for the fourth time, He promised that He would rise again (note Mark 9:9). He told His disciples the truth, but they were in no condition to understand it.

—*Be Diligent*, page 125

9. Why were the disciples having a hard time understanding Jesus' message about His coming death and resurrection? What did this reveal about their growing doubts concerning who Jesus truly was? How might this have affected their ability to minister?

From the Commentary

A large crowd of Passover pilgrims followed Jesus and His disciples to Jericho, about eighteen miles from Jerusalem. There were actually two cities named Jericho: the old city in ruins, and the new city a mile away, where Herod the Great and his successors built a lavish winter palace. This may help explain the seeming contradiction between Mark 10:46 and Luke 18:35.

There were two blind beggars sitting by the road (Matt. 20:30), one of whom was named Bartimaeus. Both Mark and Luke focused attention on him since he was the more vocal of the two. The beggars heard that Jesus of Nazareth, the Healer, was passing by; they did their best to get His attention so that they might receive His merciful help and be healed.

At first, the crowd tried to silence them, but when Jesus stopped and called for the men, the crowd encouraged them!

—*Be Diligent*, page 127

10. Review Mark 10:46–52. How would Jesus' message in this passage have been received by the Pharisees? By the common Jew who was trying to live according to the Law? By the disciples who were struggling to understand all that Jesus was teaching them? What is the message in this for our church today?

Looking Inward

Take a moment to reflect on all that you've explored thus far in this study of Mark 10. Review your notes and answers and think about how each of these things matters in your life today.

Tips for Small Groups: To get the most out of this section, form pairs or trios and have group members take turns answering these questions. Be honest and as open as you can in this discussion, but most of all, be encouraging and supportive of others. Be sensitive to those who are going through particularly difficult times and don't press for people to speak if they're uncomfortable doing so.

11. How do you feel about Jesus' use of paradoxical statements and questions as a teaching method? What makes paradoxes meaningful to you? What challenges do they bring to your understanding of what it means to grow in faith?

12. Do you ever find yourself noting wealth or possessions as evidence of God's blessing on your life? Explain. Why is this dangerous thinking? What happens when you start to base your understanding of God's blessing in terms of personal wealth or even health?

13. Are you ever tempted to pursue a good-works approach to salvation? What prompts this? What does Jesus' teaching about the rich young man say to you about the good-works approach? What does it look like, in your specific situation, to "give up everything and follow Jesus"?

Going Forward

14. Think of one or two things that you have learned that you'd like to work on in the coming week. Remember that this is all about quality, not quantity. It's better to work on one specific area of life and do it well than to work on many and do poorly (or to be so overwhelmed that you simply don't try).

Do you want to better understand Jesus' teaching on marriage? Or His teaching on what it means to be truly rich? Be specific. Go back through Mark 10 and put a star next to the phrase or verse that is most encouraging to you. Consider memorizing this verse.

Real-Life Application Ideas: If you're married, this would be the perfect time to schedule a marriage retreat. Meanwhile, start looking for ways to build your relationship with your spouse so that you have a solid foundation to withstand the inevitable difficult times that threaten all marriages. Spend more time this week listening to your spouse than talking (unless the thing your spouse longs for is your participation in conversation!).

Seeking Help

15. Write a prayer below (or simply pray one in silence), inviting God to work on your mind and heart in those areas you've noted in the Going Forward section. Be honest about your desires and fears.

Notes for Small Groups:

- *Look for ways to put into practice the things you wrote in the Going Forward section. Talk with other group members about your ideas and commit to being accountable to one another.*

- *During the coming week, ask the Holy Spirit to continue to reveal truth to you from what you've read and studied.*

- *Before you start the next lesson, read Mark 11—13. For more in-depth lesson preparation, read chapters 9 and 10, "The Servant in Jerusalem" and "The Servant Unveils the Future," in* Be Diligent.

Jerusalem
(MARK 11—13)

Before you begin ...
- *Pray for the Holy Spirit to reveal truth and wisdom as you go through this lesson.*
- *Read Mark 11—13. This lesson references chapters 9 and 10 in* Be Diligent. *It will be helpful for you to have your Bible and a copy of the commentary available as you work through this lesson.*

Getting Started

From the Commentary

On the road Jesus took, a traveler would arrive first at Bethany and then come to Bethphage, about two miles from Jerusalem. The elevation at this point is about 2,600 feet, and from it you have a breathtaking view of the Holy City. The Lord was about to do something He had never done before, something He had repeatedly cautioned others not to do for Him: He was going to permit His followers to give a public demonstration in His honor.

—*Be Diligent*, pages 131–32

1. Review Mark 11:1–11. What might have been going through Jesus' mind as He made this trek to Jerusalem? What would the disciples have been wrestling with? What might the city have looked like to them? Why do you think Jesus allowed people to celebrate Him in such a public way?

More to Consider: Jesus sent two of His disciples to Bethphage to get the colt that He needed for the event. Most people today think of a donkey as nothing but a humble beast of burden, but in that day, it was looked on as an animal fit for a king to use (1 Kings 1:33). Why did Jesus need this animal? Read Zechariah 9:9. Why didn't Mark quote this verse? (Keep in mind the audience Mark was addressing.)

2. Choose one verse or phrase from Mark 11—13 that stands out to you. This could be something you're intrigued by, something that makes you uncomfortable, something that puzzles you, something that resonates with you, or just something you want to examine further. Write that here.

Going Deeper

From the Commentary

Our Lord's condemning of the tree and cleansing of the temple (Mark 11:12–26) were both symbolic acts that illustrated the sad spiritual condition of the nation of Israel. In spite of its many privileges and opportunities, Israel was outwardly fruitless (the tree) and inwardly corrupt (the temple). It was unusual for Jesus to act in judgment (John 3:17), yet there comes a time when this is the only thing God can do (John 12:35–41).

The fig tree produces leaves in March or April and then starts to bear fruit in June, with another crop in August and possibly a third crop in December. The presence of leaves could mean the presence of fruit, even though that fruit was "left over" from the previous season. It is significant that in this instance Jesus did not have special knowledge to guide Him; He had to go to the tree and examine things for Himself.

If He had power to kill the tree, why didn't He use that power to restore the tree and make it produce fruit? Apart from the drowning of the pigs (Mark 5:13), this is the only instance of our Lord using His miraculous power to destroy something in nature. He did it because He wanted to teach us two important lessons.

—*Be Diligent*, pages 133–34

3. How was the condemning of the fig tree a lesson in failure? How was it a lesson in faith?

From the Commentary

Jesus had cleansed the temple during His first Passover visit (John 2:13–22), but the results had been temporary. It was not long before the religious leaders permitted the money changers and the merchants to return. The priests received their share of the profits, and, after all, these services were a convenience to the Jews who traveled to Jerusalem to worship. Suppose a foreign Jew carried his own sacrifice with him and then discovered that it was rejected because of some blemish? The money rates were always changing, so the men who exchanged foreign currency were doing the visitors a favor, even though the merchants were making a generous profit. It was easy for them to rationalize the whole enterprise.

This "religious market" was set up in the court of the Gentiles, the one place where the Jews should have been busy doing serious missionary work. If a Gentile visited the temple and saw what the Jews were doing *in the name of the true God*, he would never want to believe what they taught. The Jews might not have permitted idols of wood and stone in their temple, but there were idols there just the same. The court of the Gentiles should have been a place for praying, but it was instead a place for preying and paying.

—*Be Diligent*, page 136

4. How did the merchants in the temple victimize the poor? Why would this have grieved Jesus? (See Mark 12:41–44.) Why did Jesus quote Isaiah 56:7 and Jeremiah 7:11 to defend His actions?

From the Commentary

In the days that followed, the representatives of the religious and political establishment descended on Jesus as He ministered in the temple, trying their best to trip Him up with their questions. He answered four questions, and then He asked them a question that silenced them for good.

As the official guardians of the law, the members of the Sanhedrin had both the right and the responsibility to investigate anyone who claimed to be sent by God, and that included Jesus (see Deut. 18:15–22). However, these men did not have open minds or sincere motives. They were not seeking truth; they were looking for evidence to use to destroy Him (Mark 11:18). Jesus knew what they were doing, so He countered their question with another question and exposed their hypocrisy.

Why take them all the way back to John the Baptist? For a very good reason: God does not teach us new truth if we have rejected the truth He has already revealed. This basic principle is expressed in John 7:17: "If anyone is willing to do His will, he will know of the teaching, whether it is of God or whether I speak from Myself" (NASB). "Obedience is the organ of spiritual knowledge," said the British preacher F. W. Robertson. The Jewish religious leaders had not accepted what John had taught, so why should God say anything more to them? Had they obeyed John's message, they would have gladly submitted to Christ's authority, for John came to present the Messiah to the nation.

—*Be Diligent*, pages 137–38

5. Review Mark 11:27—12:12. What dilemma of their own making were the Jewish leaders caught in? How was their line of questioning akin to the approach of a hypocrite or a crowd pleaser? How did their line of questioning differ from that of Jesus (Mark 12:13–17) or John the Baptist (Matt. 11:1–10)? What did the parable Jesus told the Pharisees reveal about where their sins were leading them?

From the Commentary

Mark 12:18–27 is the only place in Mark's gospel where the Sadducees are mentioned. This group accepted only the law of Moses as their religious authority; so, if a doctrine could not be defended from the first five books of the Old Testament, they would not accept it. They did not believe in the existence of the soul, life after death, resurrection, final judgment, angels, or demons (see Acts 23:8). Most of the Sadducees were priests and were wealthy. They considered themselves the "religious aristocrats" of Judaism and tended to look down on everybody else.

They brought a hypothetical question to Jesus, based on the law of marriage given in Deuteronomy 25:7–10. This woman had a series of seven husbands during her lifetime, all brothers, and all of whom had died. "If there is such a thing as a future resurrection," they argued, "then she must spend eternity with seven husbands!" It seemed a perfect argument, as most arguments are that are based on hypothetical situations.

The Sadducees thought that they were smart, but Jesus soon revealed their ignorance of two things: the power of God and the truth of Scripture. Resurrection is not the restoration of life as we know it; it is the entrance into a new life that is different. The same God who created the angels and gave them their nature is able to give us the new bodies we will need for new life in heaven (1 Cor. 15:38ff.).

—*Be Diligent*, page 141

6. Review Mark 12:18–27. How did Jesus answer the Sadducees' question? Why would there be no need for marriage, procreation, and the continuance of the race in heaven? How was this a particularly wise answer, considering the people Jesus was answering?

From the Commentary

In Mark 12:35–37 it was our Lord's turn to ask the questions, and He focused on the most important question of all: Who is the Messiah? "What think ye of Christ? Whose Son is he?" (Matt. 22:42). This is a far more important question than the ones His enemies had asked Him, for if we are wrong about Jesus Christ, we are wrong about salvation. This means we end up condemning our own souls (John 3:16–21; 8:24; 1 John 2:18–23).

Jesus quoted Psalm 110:1 and asked them to explain how David's son could also be David's Lord. The Jews believed that the Messiah would be David's son (John 7:41–42), but the only way David's son could also be David's Lord would be if Messiah were *God come in human flesh*. The answer, of course, is our Lord's miraculous conception and virgin birth (Isa. 7:14; Matt. 1:18–25; Luke 1:26–38).

—*Be Diligent*, page 143

7. Mark 12 ends with Jesus giving two warnings (see vv. 38–40 and 41–44). What do these warnings teach us about how character is defined? Why is this important, particularly in light of where Jesus was in His ministry?

From the Commentary

The Jews were proud of their temple, in spite of the fact that it was built by the Herod family in order to placate the Jews. Jesus had already given His estimate of the temple (Mark 11:15–17), but His disciples were fascinated by the magnificence of the structure. Imagine how shocked they were when Jesus informed them that the building they admired so much would one day be demolished. The Jewish leaders had defiled it; Jesus would depart from it and leave it desolate (Matt. 23:38); the Romans would destroy it.

Once away from the crowds, Jesus' disciples asked Him when this momentous event would take place and what would happen to indicate it was soon to occur. Their questions revealed that their understanding of prophecy was still quite confused. They thought that the destruction of the temple coincided with the end of the age and the return of their Lord (Matt. 24:3). But their questions gave Jesus the opportunity to deliver a prophetic message that is generally called "The Olivet Discourse" (Matt. 24—25; Luke 21:5–36).

As we study this important sermon, we must follow some practical guidelines. To begin with, we must study this discourse in the light of the rest of Scripture, especially the book of Daniel. The prophetic Scriptures harmonize if we consider all that God has revealed.

Second, we must see the practical application of the discourse. Jesus did not preach this sermon to satisfy the curiosity of His disciples, or even to straighten out their confused thinking. At least four times He said, "Take heed!" (Mark 13:5, 9, 23, 33), and He closed the address with the admonition, "Watch!" While studying this address can help us better understand future events, we must not make the mistake of setting dates (Mark 13:32)!

Third, as we study, we must keep in mind the "Jewish atmosphere" of the discourse. The Olivet Discourse grew out of some questions asked of a Jewish rabbi by four Jewish men, about the future of the Jewish temple. The warnings about "false Christs" would especially concern Jews (Mark 13:5–6, 21–22), as would the warning about Jewish courts and trials (Mark 13:9). The Jews would especially appreciate the reference to "Daniel the prophet" and the admonition to flee from Judea (Mark 13:14).

Finally, we must remember that this chapter describes a period of time known as "the tribulation" (Mark 13:19, 24; also see Matt. 24:21, 29). The Old Testament prophets wrote about this period and called it "the time of Jacob's trouble" (Jer. 30:7), a time of wrath (Zeph. 1:15–18), and a time of indignation and punishment (Isa. 26:20–21). As we shall see, it is Daniel the prophet who gives us the "key," resulting in a better understanding of the sequence of events.

—*Be Diligent*, pages 147–48

8. Why did Jesus take the time to talk about the destruction of the temple and what it meant? In what ways would this discourse have satisfied Jesus' followers? In what ways might it have left them even more confused? How does Mark 13 show us Jesus the Prophet as well as Jesus the Servant?

More to Consider: In Mark 13, Jesus described three stages in this tribulation period: (1) the beginning (Mark 13:5–13); (2) the middle (Mark 13:14–18); and (3) the events that lead to the end (Mark 13:19–27). What do the two parables that follow this description teach us about how we're to respond to these prophecies? (See Mark 13:28–37.) Compare this section to Matthew's account (Matt. 24). Keep in mind the different audiences each writer wrote to (Mark: the Romans; Matthew: the Jews).

From the Commentary

There is a key statement at the end of Mark 13:8: "These are the beginnings of sorrows." The word translated "sorrows" means "birth pangs," suggesting that the world at that time will be like a woman in travail (see Isa. 13:6–8; Jer. 4:31; 6:24; 13:21; 22:20–23; 1 Thess. 5:3). The birth pangs will come suddenly, build up gradually, and lead to a time of terrible sorrow and tribulation for the whole world.

Jesus listed the things that must *not* be taken as the "signs" of His coming. Rather, they are indications that the tribulation "birth pangs" are just beginning. These signs are the success of false Christs (Mark 13:5–6), nations in conflict (Mark 13:7–8a), natural disturbances (Mark 13:8b), and religious persecutions (Mark 13:9–13). They have always been with us, but since these events are compared to "birth pangs," our Lord may be saying that *an acceleration of these things* would be significant.

False messiahs. The pages of history are filled with the tragic stories of false messiahs, false prophets, and their enthusiastic but deluded disciples.

—*Be Diligent,* page 149

9. Read Matthew 7:15–20; Acts 20:28–31; and 1 John 4:1–6. How does each of these passages warn about false prophets? Why do people so quickly choose to follow false prophets, despite the lessons of the past? How does the following idea by Mark Twain apply here: A lie runs around the world while Truth is putting on her shoes?

From the Commentary

The parable of the fig tree cautions tribulation saints to watch and to know the "signs of the times." But the parable of the householder warns *all of us today* (Mark 13:37) to be alert, because we do not know when He will return to take us to heaven (1 Cor. 15:51–52). Like the householder in the story, before our Lord went from us back to heaven, He gave each of us work to do. He expects us to be faithful while He is gone and to be working when He returns. "Take heed, watch and pray" is His admonition.

To "watch" means to be alert, to stay at one's best, to stay awake. (The English name "Gregory" comes from this Greek word translated "watch.") Why must we stay alert? Because nobody knows when Jesus Christ will return. When He was on earth in His humiliation, Jesus did not know the day or hour of His coming again. Even the angels do not know. The unsaved world scoffs at us because we continue to cling to this "blessed hope," but He will return as He promised (2 Peter 3). Our task is to be faithful and to be busy, not to speculate or debate about the hidden details of prophecy.

The Christians who read Mark's gospel eventually had to face intense persecution from Rome (1 Peter 4:12ff.), and this particular message must have brought comfort and strength to them. After all, if God is able to help His people witness during the great tribulation, the worst persecution of all, then surely He could strengthen the saints in the Roman Empire as they faced their fiery trial.

—*Be Diligent*, pages 156–57

10. How does Matthew 25:14–30 depict watchfulness? What might it look like today to put this into practice? How is this different from earning one's way into heaven? (See Eph. 2:8–10.) What sorts of persecution and tribulation might Christians today experience before Jesus returns? (See John 16:33; Acts 14:22.) How do the warnings of Mark 13 apply to us today?

Looking Inward

Take a moment to reflect on all that you've explored thus far in this study of Mark 11—13. Review your notes and answers and think about how each of these things matters in your life today.

Tips for Small Groups: To get the most out of this section, form pairs or trios and have group members take turns answering these questions. Be honest and as open as you can in this discussion, but most of all, be encouraging and supportive of others. Be sensitive to those who are going through particularly difficult times and don't press for people to speak if they're uncomfortable doing so.

11. What sorts of questions do you ask Jesus? Have you ever found yourself demanding answers from Him without a truly open heart? Why did you do that? How is this like the way the Pharisees and Sadducees approached Jesus? What does it mean to approach Jesus with an open heart? How can you do that in your faith life today?

12. How sure are you about the way the world will end? About the events described in the Gospels (and Daniel and the book of Revelation)? Is it important for you to understand these events? Why or why not?

13. What does it mean for you to be watchful in anticipation of Jesus' return? How does this affect your daily life? What are the dangers of simply watching for signs and not living in the real world as Jesus commanded?

Going Forward

14. Think of one or two things that you have learned that you'd like to work on in the coming week. Remember that this is all about quality, not quantity. It's better to work on one specific area of life and do it well than to work on many and do poorly (or to be so overwhelmed that you simply don't try).

Do you want to learn how to be more watchful in your daily life? Be specific. Go back through Mark 11—13 and put a star next to the phrase or verse that is most encouraging to you. Consider memorizing this verse.

Real-Life Application Ideas: While studying the end times can be a positive, inspiring experience, it can also leave you feeling a bit confused or frustrated. The most important message in this part of Mark's gospel is that of being watchful and avoiding false prophets. Take a look at your current faith life—how you go about growing your faith, living it, sharing it with others. Is there an element of watchfulness in it? What would it look like to be more sensitive to this kind of thinking? Look for ways to develop a watchful attitude in all aspects of your life.

Seeking Help

15. Write a prayer below (or simply pray one in silence), inviting God to work on your mind and heart in those areas you've noted in the Going Forward section. Be honest about your desires and fears.

Notes for Small Groups:

- *Look for ways to put into practice the things you wrote in the Going Forward section. Talk with other group members about your ideas and commit to being accountable to one another.*

- *During the coming week, ask the Holy Spirit to continue to reveal truth to you from what you've read and studied.*

- *Before you start the next lesson, read Mark 14—16. For more in-depth lesson preparation, read chapters 11 and 12, "The Servant Suffers" and "The Servant Finishes His Work," in* Be Diligent.

Suffering and Sacrifice
(MARK 14—16)

Before you begin …
- *Pray for the Holy Spirit to reveal truth and wisdom as you go through this lesson.*
- *Read Mark 14—16. This lesson references chapters 11 and 12 in* Be Diligent. *It will be helpful for you to have your Bible and a copy of the commentary available as you work through this lesson.*

Getting Started

From the Commentary

Mary's anointing of the Lord in Mark 14 must not be confused with a similar event recorded in Luke 7:36–50. The unnamed woman in the house of Simon the Pharisee was a converted harlot who expressed her love to Christ because of His gracious forgiveness of her many sins. In the house of Simon the (healed) leper, Mary expressed her love to Christ because He was going to the cross to die for her. She prepared His body for burial as she anointed His head (Mark 14:3) and His feet (John 12:3). She showed her love for Jesus while He was still alive.

It was an expensive offering that she gave to the Lord. Spikenard was imported from India, and a whole jar would have cost the equivalent of a common worker's annual income. Mary gave lavishly and lovingly. She was not ashamed to show her love for Christ openly.

—*Be Diligent*, page 162

1. What were the consequences of Mary's act of worship? How did the disciples respond? What was Jesus' response? What lesson did Jesus teach His disciples through this event?

More to Consider: Read John 12:1–11, then contrast Mary and Judas. Why was Judas's complaint about Mary's gift notable? How did his words provide foreshadowing for what is to come?

2. Choose one verse or phrase from Mark 14—16 that stands out to you. This could be something you're intrigued by, something that makes you

uncomfortable, something that puzzles you, something that resonates with you, or just something you want to examine further. Write that here.

Going Deeper

From the Commentary

> The Passover lamb was selected on the tenth day of the month of Nisan (our March-April), examined for blemishes, and then slain on the fourteenth day of the month (Ex. 12:3–6). The lamb had to be slain in the temple precincts and the supper eaten within the Jerusalem city limits. For the Jews, the Passover feast was the memorial of a past victory, but Jesus would institute a new supper that would be the memorial of His death.
>
> Peter and John saw to it that the supper was prepared (Luke 22:8). It would not be difficult to locate the man carrying the jar of water because the women usually performed this task. Was this man John Mark's father? Did Jesus eat the Passover in an upper room in John Mark's home? These are fascinating speculations, but we have no evidence that can confirm them. However, we do know

that John Mark's home was a center for Christian fellowship in Jerusalem (Acts 12:12).

—*Be Diligent*, page 163

3. Review Mark 14:12–26. Why is the upper room event appropriately referred to as the Last Supper? Why would Jesus choose to use such a time (the Passover feast) to tell His disciples what was to come? Why would He make Himself so available to Judas's scheming?

From the Commentary

After Judas left the scene, Jesus instituted what Christians commonly call "the Lord's Supper" or "the Eucharist." (The word *Eucharist* comes from a Greek word which means "to give thanks.") Before the cup, Jesus took one of the unleavened loaves, blessed it, broke it, and told the men, "This is My body." He then took the Passover cup, blessed it, and gave it to them, saying, "This is my blood" (see 1 Cor. 11:23–26).

Bread and wine were two common items that were used at practically every meal, but Jesus gave them a wonderful new meaning. When Jesus said "This is My body" and "This is My blood," He did not transform either the bread or the wine into anything different. When the disciples ate the bread, it was still bread; when they drank the wine, it was still wine. However, the Lord gave a new meaning to the bread and the wine, so that, from that hour, they would serve as memorials of His death.

What, then, did Jesus accomplish by His death? On the cross, Jesus fulfilled the old covenant and established a new covenant (Heb. 9—10). The old covenant was ratified with the blood of animal sacrifices, but the new covenant was ratified by the blood of God's Son. The new covenant in His blood would do what the old covenant sacrifices could not do—take away sin and cleanse the heart and conscience of the believer. We are not saved from our sins by participating in a religious ceremony, but by trusting Jesus Christ as our Savior.

Our Lord's command was, "This do in remembrance of me" (1 Cor. 11:24–25). The word translated "remembrance" means much more than "in memory of," for you can do something in memory of a dead person—yet Jesus is alive! The word carries the idea of a present participation in a past event. Because Jesus is alive, as we celebrate the Lord's Supper, by faith we have communion with Him (1 Cor. 10:16–17).

—*Be Diligent*, pages 165–66

4. Do you think it is significant that Judas didn't get to experience the Lord's Supper? Why or why not? In what ways is the Lord's Supper a spiritual experience? (See 1 Cor. 11:27–34.)

From the Commentary

On the way to the garden of Gethsemane ("oil press"), Jesus warned the disciples that they would all forsake Him, but He then assured them that He would meet them again in Galilee after His resurrection. He even quoted Zechariah 13:7—"Smite the shepherd, and the sheep shall be scattered"—to back up His warning. Their minds and hearts were unable to receive and retain His words, for three days later, they did not believe the reports of His resurrection! And the angel had to give them a special reminder to meet Him in Galilee (Mark 16:6–7). Had they listened to His word and believed it, they would have saved themselves a great deal of anxiety, and Peter would not have denied the Lord.

The quotation from Zechariah told the disciples what to do when the Jews arrested Jesus: *scatter!* In fact, at the very time of His arrest, Jesus said, "Let these [disciples] go their way" (John 18:8). In other words, "Men, get out of here!" I have read eloquent sermons blaming Peter for "following afar off," but they completely miss the point. He was not supposed to follow at all! Had he obeyed the Lord, he would not have attacked a man with his sword or denied the Lord three times.

—*Be Diligent*, pages 166–67

5. Review Mark 14:27–52. Why did Peter have a hard time applying Jesus' commands to himself? Read John 18:1–11. What was Peter's instinct when Jesus was arrested? Why was this the wrong thing to do?

From the Commentary

Both the Jewish trial and the Roman trial were in three stages. The Jewish trial was opened by Annas, the former high priest (John 18:13–24). It then moved to the full council to hear witnesses (Mark 14:53–65), and then to an early morning session for the final vote of condemnation (Mark 15:1). Jesus was then sent to Pilate (Mark 15:1–5; John 18:28–38), who sent Him to Herod (Luke

23:6–12), who returned Him to Pilate (Mark 15:6–15; John 18:39—19:6). Pilate yielded to the cry of the mob and delivered Jesus to be crucified.

By the time the soldiers arrived at the palace of the high priest, Peter and John, heedless of the Lord's repeated warnings, followed the mob and even went into the courtyard. Jesus that night had sweat "as it were great drops of blood" (Luke 22:44), but Peter was cold and sat by the enemy fire! The two disciples could not witness the actual trial, but at least they were near enough to see the outcome (Matt. 26:58; John 18:15).

After questioning and insulting Jesus, Annas sent Jesus bound to his son-in-law Caiaphas, the high priest. The Sanhedrin was assembled and the witnesses were ready. It was necessary to have at least two witnesses before the accused could be declared guilty and worthy of death (Deut. 17:6). Many witnesses testified against Jesus, but since they did not agree, their testimony was invalid. How tragic that a group of religious leaders would encourage people to lie, and during a special holy season!

—*Be Diligent*, pages 169–70

6. How must Jesus' disciples have felt during these trials? Why did they still have a hard time doing what Jesus had told them to do? What does this say about their understanding of Jesus' teaching?

From the Commentary

Three specific hours are mentioned in this section of Mark: the third (Mark 15:25), the sixth (Mark 15:33), and the ninth (Mark 15:33–34). The Jews reckoned time from 6:00 a.m. to 6:00 p.m., so this means that the third hour was 9:00 a.m., the sixth hour noon, and the ninth hour 3:00 p.m. Mark followed the Jewish system, whereas the apostle John used Roman time in his gospel. This means that "the sixth hour" in John 19:14 is 6:00 a.m.

The third hour (Mark 15:21–32). According to law, the guilty victim had to carry his cross, or at least the crossbeam, to the place of execution, and Jesus was no exception. He left Pilate's hall bearing His cross (John 19:16–17), but He could not continue, so the soldiers "drafted" Simon of Cyrene to carry the cross for Him. Roman officers had the privilege of "impressing" men for service, and the way they used this privilege irritated the Jews (Matt. 5:41).

The sixth hour (Mark 15:33). At noon, a miraculous darkness came over the land, and all creation sympathized with the Creator as He suffered. This was indeed a miracle and not some natural phenomenon, such as a sand storm or an eclipse. It would not be possible to have an eclipse during full moon at Passover. By means of this darkness, God was saying something to the people.

The ninth hour (Mark 15:34–41). Our Lord made seven statements from the cross, three of them before the darkness came: "Father, forgive them; for they know not what they do" (Luke 23:34); "Today shalt thou be with me in paradise" (Luke 23:43); and "Woman, behold thy son.... Behold thy mother" (John 19:26–27). When the darkness came, there was silence on His cross, for it was then that He was made sin for us (2 Cor. 5:21).

—*Be Diligent*, pages 177–78, 80–81

7. Review Mark 15:21–41. Why do you think Mark mentioned the particular hours? What does this part of the narrative reveal about Jesus' crucifixion? About the sudden changes Jesus' disciples had to deal with? What does the speed of this event teach us about the fears of the Jewish leaders? The Roman officials?

From the Commentary

The Jews recognized two evenings: "early evening" from three to six o'clock, and "evening" after six o'clock, when the new day would begin. This explains how both Matthew (27:57) and Mark (15:42) could call late Friday afternoon "evening." It was important that the place of execution be quickly cleared, because the Jewish Sabbath was about to begin, and that Sabbath was a "high day" because of the Passover (John 19:31).

God had a wealthy member of the Sanhedrin, Joseph of Arimathea, ready to take care of the body of Jesus (Matt. 27:57). He was assisted by Nicodemus, also a member of the council (John 19:38–42). We must not think that these two men suddenly decided to bury Jesus, because what they did demanded much preparation.

To begin with, Joseph had to prepare the tomb in a garden near the place where Jesus died. This tomb was probably not for Joseph himself, since a wealthy man would not likely choose to be buried near a place of execution. The men also had to obtain a large quantity of spices (John 19:39), and this could not be done when the shops were closed for Passover. And all of this had to be done without the council's knowledge.

—*Be Diligent*, page 182

8. Review Mark 15:42–47. How important was Joseph of Arimathea's role in the overall story of Jesus' burial? Why do you think he was mentioned in the Scriptures? What does his preparation say about how some people valued Jesus? Where do you see God's planning in this part of the story?

More to Consider: Why was it important that Jesus' body be prepared for burial? (See John 20:1–9.) How does this fulfill the prophecy in Isaiah 53:9? Why was it important that Jesus was buried at all?

From the Commentary

Jesus Christ was "delivered for our offenses, and was raised again for our justification" (Rom. 4:25). A dead Savior cannot save anybody. The resurrection of Jesus Christ from the dead is as much a part of the gospel message as His sacrificial death on the cross (1 Cor. 15:1–8). In fact, in the book of Acts, the church gave witness primarily to the resurrection (Acts 1:22; 4:2, 33).

Jesus had told His disciples that He would be raised from the dead, but they had not grasped the meaning of this truth (Mark 9:9–10, 31; 10:34). Even the women who came early to the tomb did not expect to see Him alive. In fact, they had purchased spices to complete the anointing that Joseph and Nicodemus had so hastily begun.

When you combine the accounts in the Gospels, you arrive at the following probable order of resurrection appearances on that first day of the week: (1) to Mary Magdalene (John 20:11–18 and Mark 16:9–11); (2) to the other women (Matt. 28:9–10); (3) to Peter (Luke 24:34 and 1 Cor. 15:5); (4) to the two men going to Emmaus (Mark 16:12 and Luke 24:13–32); and (5) to ten of the disciples in the upper room (Mark 16:14 and John 20:19–25).

—*Be Diligent*, pages 183–84

9. How does the resurrection prove that Jesus is who He claimed to be? Review the five appearances of Jesus (as noted in the previous commentary excerpt). How do these contribute to the evidence that Jesus rose from the dead? What are the significances of each appearance?

From the Commentary

Both Paul and Mark emphasize the need for God's people to get the message out to all nations (Mark 16:15–16; Phil. 2:10–11), and there is the added assurance that God is at work in and through them (Mark 16:19–20; Phil. 2:12–13).

One of Jesus' heavenly ministries is that of enabling His people to do His will (Heb. 13:20–21). It is fitting that the gospel of the Servant should end with this reference to work, just as it is fitting for Matthew, the gospel of the King, to end with a reference to His great authority. By His Holy Spirit, the Lord wants to work *in* us (Phil. 2:12–13), *with* us (Mark 16:20), and *for* us (Rom. 8:28).

—*Be Diligent,* page 187

10. Review Mark 16:19–20. How does this passage parallel Philippians 2:9? How does Jesus' ascension mark the completion of His earthly ministry? What is the significance of the ascension?

Looking Inward

Take a moment to reflect on all that you've explored thus far in this study of Mark 14—16. Review your notes and answers and think about how each of these things matters in your life today.

> *Tips for Small Groups: To get the most out of this section, form pairs or trios and have group members take turns answering these questions. Be honest and as open as you can in this discussion, but most of all, be encouraging and supportive of others. Be sensitive to those who are going through particularly difficult times and don't press for people to speak if they're uncomfortable doing so.*

11. What are some ways that you have generously given to God as Mary did when she anointed Jesus with oil? What are some of the ways you've been tempted to deny Jesus like Peter did?

12. How does the crucifixion story make you feel? What are some ways you relate to the disciples who were struggling with how to respond to Jesus' trials and death on the cross? Because we have the benefit of history, we know Jesus rose from the dead. But how would you have felt if you didn't know Jesus would rise from the dead?

13. How does Jesus' resurrection affect your daily faith life? What does it mean to you personally?

Going Forward

14. Think of one or two things that you have learned that you'd like to work on in the coming week. Remember that this is all about quality, not quantity. It's better to work on one specific area of life and do it well than to work on many and do poorly (or to be so overwhelmed that you simply don't try).

Do you want to learn how to embrace the resurrection story in daily life? Be specific. Go back through Mark 14—16 and put a star next to the phrase or verse that is most encouraging to you. Consider memorizing this verse.

Real-Life Application Ideas: The climax of Jesus' story as told in the book of Mark comes not at His death, but with His resurrection. It is because Jesus conquered death that we can have forgiveness for sins and the promise of new life to come. This is the best news ever! This week, celebrate Jesus' sacrifice and look for every opportunity to share the good news with friends who don't yet know Jesus.

Seeking Help

15. Write a prayer below (or simply pray one in silence), inviting God to work on your mind and heart in those areas you've noted in the Going Forward section. Be honest about your desires and fears.

Notes for Small Groups:

- *Look for ways to put into practice the things you wrote in the Going Forward section. Talk with other group members about your ideas and commit to being accountable to one another.*

- *During the coming week, ask the Holy Spirit to continue to reveal truth to you from what you've read and studied.*

Summary and Review

Notes for Small Groups: This session is a summary and review of this book. Because of that, it is shorter than the previous lessons. If you are using this in a small-group setting, consider combining this lesson with a time of fellowship or a shared meal.

> *Before you begin ...*
> - *Pray for the Holy Spirit to reveal truth and wisdom as you go through this lesson.*
> - *Briefly review the notes you made in the previous sessions. You will refer back to previous sections throughout this bonus lesson.*

Looking Back

1. Over the past eight lessons, you've examined Jesus' life, death, and resurrection. What expectations did you bring to this study? In what ways were those expectations met?

2. What is the most significant personal discovery you've made from this study?

3. What surprised you most about Mark's gospel? What, if anything, troubled you?

Progress Report

4. Take a few moments to review the Going Forward sections of the previous lessons. How would you rate your progress for each of the things you chose to work on? What adjustments, if any, do you need to make to continue on the path toward spiritual maturity?

5. In what ways have you grown closer to Christ during this study? Take a moment to celebrate those things. Then think of areas where you feel you still need to grow and note those here. Make plans to revisit this study in a few weeks to review your growing faith.

Things to Pray About

6. Mark's gospel is a book that celebrates Jesus as the Servant of all. As you reflect on Jesus' servant role, think about how this affects your daily life.

7. The messages in Mark's gospel include trust, unbelief, and following Jesus even unto death. Spend time praying about each of these topics.

8. Whether you've been studying this in a small group or on your own, there are many other Christians working through the very same issues you discovered when examining Mark's gospel. Take time to pray for them, that God would reveal truth, that the Holy Spirit would guide you, and that each person might grow in spiritual maturity according to God's will.

A Blessing of Encouragement

Studying the Bible is one of the best ways to learn how to be more like Christ. Thanks for taking this step. In closing, let this blessing precede you and follow you into the next week while you continue to marinate in God's Word:

May God light your path to greater understanding as you review the truths found in the book of Mark and consider how they can help you grow closer to Christ.

The "BE" series . . .

For years pastors and lay leaders have embraced Warren W. Wiersbe's very accessible commentary of the Bible through the individual "BE" series. Through the work of David C. Cook Global Mission, the "BE" series is part of a library of books made available to indigenous Christian workers. These are men and women who are called by God to grow the kingdom through their work with the local church worldwide. Here are a few of their remarks as to how Dr. Wiersbe's writings have benefited their ministry.

"Most Christian books I see are priced too high for me . . .
I received a collection that included 12 Wiersbe
commentaries a few months ago and I have
read every one of them.
I use them for my personal devotions every day and they
are incredibly helpful for preparing sermons.
The contribution David C. Cook is making to the
church in India is amazing."
—Pastor E. M. Abraham, Hyderabad, India

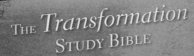